I thank my God for all the
memories I have of you.
Every time I pray for all of you,
I do it with joy . . .
You have a special place in my heart.

Philippians 1: 3,4 & 7a   (GOD'S WORD)

Sincere Appreciation Is Extended To

ART ATTACK CREATIVE, INC.
Colorado Springs, Colorado

Roald Ramsey,
Mun Choi & Craig Torstenbo

❧❧

Special Thanks To

Marshall Goin

For His Encouraging Words

The Tie That Binds

JAN KELLER

৵৶

Edited by
Janetta Roberts

Black Sheep Books
& Publishing

P.O. Box 325
Calhan, CO 80808

Cover design by Mun Choi, Art Director
Art Attack Creative, Inc., Colorado Springs, CO.

Cover photo by Owen Riss.

Back cover photo by Tom Kimmell.

Text author photo by Janet Mock.

Book text design, layout, typography and text photos by Jan Keller.

Quilted heart pictured on cover crafted by Sandra Erickson.

Quilt pictured on cover by Jan Keller's fraternal grandmother, Kathryn Goldsmith.

Manufactured in the United States of America.

First Edition
First Printing

ACKNOWLEDGEMENTS
Kim Bass,
John Keller, Mickey Keller, Maury Keller, Lana Keller, Millie Frank,
Bill Bruhn, Kedrann Dotson, Phyllis Erickson, Scott Fortney,
Becky Gaddy, Monty Gaddy, Eli Gerson, Doris Heine, Louise Holcomb,
Dee Martz, Janet Mock, Vicki Nelson, Minh Nguyen and Dawn Walker

Publisher's Cataloging-in-Publication
(Provided by Quality Books, Inc.)

Keller, Jan (Janice)
    The tie that binds / Jan Kellar ; edited by Janetta
Roberts. -- 1st ed.
    p. cm.
    ISBN: 1-889579-97-1
    1. Love. 2. Love--Anecdotes. 3. Interpersonal
relations--Anecdotes. 4. Family--Anecdotes.   I. Robert
Janetta. II. Title.
BF575.L8K45 1998   152.4'1
                                    QBI98-253

In Memory Of

Amber Adele Fetters

July 31, 1977 – July 1, 1995

Dear Reader,

When the word power is verbalized, we each come up with a unique and varied mental image. When I hear the word power, I think about a July sky that darkened very quickly with turbulent storm clouds. The first lightning bolt was furiously hurled at an unsuspecting blithe and beautiful seventeen-year-old woman who was enjoying God's grand and glorious out-of-doors by playing golf with her mother and boyfriend. Because the storm developed so quickly, the warning sirens sounded only after the first violent strike.

The young woman's name was Amber, and her boyfriend was my youngest son Mick. Amber had just completed her senior year of high school by taking classes at a nearby University. Only a few days earlier she had stood tall and proud behind the podium, speaking at her high school graduation, and challenging her classmates with the charge to, quote, "Go and grow!"

July was supposed to be the month when she would celebrate her eighteenth birthday. Instead, Amber received a jolt so powerful it threw her to the ground and unceremoniously ended her life before it hardly began.

In the days and weeks that followed, good people who meant well said things like, "It was God's will," or "God takes the best home first," or "It was Amber's time, and someday we'd understand." But I didn't find consolation in their words. Instead, I was comforted by the memory of a friend and cancer victim who, in the midst of her battle, had told me, "God doesn't control everything that happens to us, but He gives us the power to deal with it after it happens."

Whether by accident, illness, death or despair, who hasn't been struck by some devastating bolt out of the blue? To live is to love, and to love is to ultimately suffer and endure loss. Life, by its very nature, brings heartache and pain. And though this is the human condition, life's traumas and dramas, though used by God, are not necessarily acts of God. Luke 9: 51-55 says:

The time was coming closer for Jesus to be taken to heaven. So he was determined to go to Jerusalem. He sent messengers ahead of him. They went into a Samaritan village to arrange a place for him to stay. But the people didn't welcome him, because he was on his way to Jerusalem. James and John, his disciples, saw this. They asked, "Lord, do you want us to call down fire form heaven to burn them up?"

But he turned and corrected them.   (GOD'S WORD)

On Palm Sunday the following April, I spent the afternoon working in the yard, raking away last year's dead and decaying debris. As I carefully tended the area beneath the beautiful and graceful weeping birch tree we planted as a living memorial to Amber, I delighted in the discovery of Spring's first life-affirming bulbs growing and blooming at its base.

Through a stream of tears, I looked at the bright beauty of the blossoms and reflected on Amber's charge to, "Go and grow!" Slowly, a bittersweet smile spread across my face as I realized, when God is the source of our power, as survivors of life's harsh and difficult seasons of winter, like the bulb, we too can spring forth and bloom.

I challenge you to, "Go and grow."

Love,

Jan Keller

CONTENTS

CONTENTS

❧ The Tie That Binds ❧

To everything there is a season, and a time for every purpose under heaven:
    a time to be born and a time to die,
    a time to plant and a time to harvest,
    a time to kill and a time to heal,
    a time to destroy and a time to rebuild,
    a time to cry and a time to laugh,
    a time to grieve and a time to dance,
    a time to scatter stones and time to gather stones,
    a time to embrace and a time to refrain from embracing,
    a time to find and a time to lose,
    a time to keep and a time to throw away,
    a time to tear and a time to mend,
    a time to be silent and a time to speak,
    a time to love and a time to hate,
    a time for war and a time for peace.   *Ecclesiastes 3: 1-8*

There you have it -- the story of my life.
Those eight Biblical verses are also the story of your life -- as well as the simple generic story of *every* person who ever lived.

Although those verses are beautiful and treasured, when desiring to know and understand a specific person, they aren't enough.

Usually it is sufficient to connect with a person and travel from that point on together, sharing a present and a future, that ultimately become their common past. For me and my friend Janet, however, that wasn't enough. We decided to take time to spend a weekend discovering and bonding our pasts so we could better understand the environment and events that shaped us into the women we have become.

Janet and I became friends when our children were teenagers. Even though we settled and raised our children in different communities, we discovered we had a great deal in common. I was born first, but before a year had past, she too made her arrival. Both of us grew up on farms near Greeley, Colorado and must have unknowingly competed against each other at the county fair with various 4-H projects. She married first; but less than a year later, I followed her down the aisle. We each had two children. The oldest are about the same age, as are the youngest.

During our special weekend, we toured the farms where we were raised, driving past former schools, meeting relatives and sharing meals with each other's parents. By observing family interactions, we gained keener and clearer perceptions of the influences and values that formed the other.

The similarities in our backgrounds are striking, yet, this nostalgic trip also brought our differences into focus. Both of us went roller skating at the same rink. Both of us fell and broke an arm. Both of us had to learn to write with our alternate hand. But, she broke her right arm. I broke my left. I continued to love to skate. She didn't.

My friend and I will travel on together, sharing the present and the future more completely because we took time to take a peek at the past. We've transformed generic existence into a rich and complex tapestry of unique scenes and experiences and can view the other and more fully appreciate all the variations in color and texture.

In spite of individual diversity, *all* will experience birth, love and laughter as well as hate, greed and grief. *None* experience anything really new or that hasn't ever happened before.

The ultimate tie that binds is the reality everyone who has a time to be born also has a time to die.

It is probably absurd vanity to think the specifics of any life to be of consequence — but for me, having a friend who knows, cares, and understands has made a difference.

~ The Magical Mystery Boxes ~

I was recently given three magical mystery boxes . . . and just in time for the holidays!

One of the boxes was very small, another medium sized, and the third was large. Very large. As large as I want it to be.

These boxes, though imaginary, proved to be a mind-blowing exercise in fantasy because they came with the instructions to fill them with gifts to myself. Absolutely *anything* my wild imaginings could conjure!

Receiving these boxes is a bit like an adult climbing onto Santa's lap. At first I didn't fit because I'm more accustomed to thinking about what my children or husband want or need. It felt strange to focus, instead, on what I might like or what would be good for me.

As a child, I wanted a Betsy Wetsy doll more than anything else in the whole wide world. Back then, my wants were simple and Santa usually could make my dreams come true. As an adult, there aren't too many *things* I want badly enough to utilize a magical mystery box so valuable as these. Most of the current desires of my heart, though tangible, are not material in nature.

Should a hug shared with a loved one fill my tiny box? Might I like to surround myself in the aroma of a batch of baking cookies, with the extra bonus of being able to give some as a gift to a friend? A fun family evening of playing games together might be a nice choice. Or, might I rather fill the little box with a totally happy day?

Such decisions!

I have trouble thinking of medium sized desires, but some of my ideas include going back to college or being totally debt-free.

Finally there's the box as big and expansive as I want or can imagine it to be. I could fill it with wonderful relationships, a fulfilling life, or a series of new and challenging experiences that would keep me physically and mentally vital and alive.

Which should I choose?

The choice is all mine!

These three boxes have been a wonderful gift, causing me to realize *I* am the key to most of my desires. Only I can turn these heart-held longings into reality. I simply have to decide if I want one or all of my desires enough to work for their realization and accomplishment.

I can share a hug, bake a batch of cookies, spend a fun evening with my family, or simply decide to be totally happy for a whole day. I also could, through effort, become debt-free or return to college. Having wonderful relationships throughout a challenging, fulfilling and vital life is my option.

The choice is mine -- and yours.

It's yours because I'm giving you the same three magical mystery boxes, covered with bright wrapping and beautiful satin bows, along with the challenge to fill them with your heart's desires.

Dare to make your dreams come true while enjoying the most wonderful holiday season ever!

Growing Into Dad's Shoes

"Yea! Two points!" exclaimed our pre-school-age sons, who were engrossed in their serious game of kitchen basketball. The hoop, attached to the refrigerator by suction cups, was strategically located at the appropriate height to allow these pint-sized hoopsters to dunk the ball.

They idolized their dad and wanted to be just like him. Their interactions with him were highlights, filled with the imperceptible important lessons best taught by example.

To make play time more fulfilling, they carried Dad's duffel bag into the kitchen and wore one of Dad's town team uniforms.

It was important the hoop not be too high because, as one hand directed the scaled-down ball to score, the other hand was needed to hold up Dad's trunks. Guarding wasn't any easier because one hand had to hang on to the shoulder straps of Dad's numbered top to keep it from dropping off the shoulder and falling to the floor.

Nothing fit, and the shoes, countless sizes too large, hindered the little men from making smooth moves. But it didn't matter. Nothing could have been any more important than attempting to be just like Dad!

❧❧

"Hey Dad, can I borrow your sport coat? Where are your matching argyle socks? I sure hope you haven't worn them!"

The coat fits, the socks are located, and it's the day of a big game. Only now our sons are the players and Dad increasingly joins the bleacher brigade as spectator and fan.

"To everything there is a season" . . . And now, sometimes, it's Dad who is borrowing his son's knit top or sweater.

The boys, striving for independence, have developed distinct individual personalities; but they've unwittingly learned, by observation, the lessons Dad taught by example.

There was a time, a brief time, when the boys could wear Dad's shoes; but the fit was never perfect. Those days are gone and now it's necessary for the boys to go their own way, wearing their own shoes.

✎ Wash Day Blues ❧

*D*oing the laundry is not my favorite chore. Nor is it one from which I derive a great sense of self-worth. Washing soiled clothes is a dirty and sometimes smelly routine job. It's easily taken for granted and often only noticed when it isn't done. But, somebody's got to do it!

Everybody at our house could wash the clothes, but usually it's my job. To simplify the task, I have four large wastebaskets strategically located in the closet in the boy's bathroom. Each wastebasket is labeled (white, jeans, colored, or dress), and everyone does their own sorting, dividing their clothes into the proper container. This system works well for me because when any wastebasket is full, I know it's time . . .

Everyone knows to empty their pockets so everything's ready to swish and spin. If money is left in a pocket, I find it after it's been washed and assume it's my tip. Occasionally a tube of red, cherry flavored Chap-Stick gets washed and rinsed along with a load of clothes. As I transfer the resulting pink-spotted clean clothes into the dryer, I console myself with the knowledge it's not my fault.

The only exception is athletic uniforms. They have to be ready by the next game day, so they're to be placed on top of the washer, where I can't miss them.

The biggest washing challenge I've come up against is football uniforms! The real contest isn't the head-to-head confrontation of the players on the field, but removing the blood, sweat, grime and grass stains.

No mother wants to send her son back onto the playing field, and into the careful scrutiny of every other mother, in anything less than a dazzling bright and clean uniform. Talk about a keen 'clean' competition!

I first accepted the uniform challenge when my oldest son, Maury, started playing junior high football. This year he's a senior, so, for the past six years, washing football uniforms has been routine.

Now that this year's final game has been played, one last time, I loaded the washer -- the very same washing machine that washed his diapers when he was an infant, and, for the final time, I washed Maury's #10 Calhan blue and white uniform, trimmed with a bit of red.

A season of his life is over. Gone. Finished.

As the water drained, I cried.

❧ *Unpacking Memories* ❧

"*M*om, do you want *this* hung on the Christmas tree?" asked one of my sons, referring to a multicolored, yarn covered triangle with no obvious commercial beauty or value.

"Yes!" I replied. "Your brother made it for me when he was in first grade."

"Yeah, *I* made that!" replied my other son, quite proudly, as he took the ornament and found a prominent tree branch where his handiwork would once again be displayed.

We carelessly toss many of our decorations into a box for storage, but the special, precious treasures, given as a token of love from family or friends, are carefully and individually wrapped prior to storage.

Every year the sentimental value of these special ornaments increases, as does the joy I experience as I annually rediscover them.

I love unpacking the pair of white kissing angels. They were purchased the first year John and I were married. They've adorned our home every Christmas since.

Last year my sister gave me a tiny baby Jesus being worshipped by a solitary black sheep. I love the symbolism of this unusual miniature crèche.

My mother has sent both of my sons an ornament every year since they were born. Their collection has grown so large that when they marry and decorate a tree in their own home, my tree will look bare.

When John's parents traveled to Hawaii, they brought me an ornament featuring a bright red tropical flower. Every year I place it where I can look at it often and be reminded of their love.

My holiday delight is dampened, however. Many years ago a friend gave me a set of plaster tree ornaments which she had hand-painted. I considered them very special and treated them with care through several holiday seasons. But then something happened and the friendship was gone.

For a couple of years after the death of this relationship, I continued to hang the ornaments because the memory of our friendship remained precious, though painful. Then, for several

Yuletides, I chose to leave them carefully packed away, supposedly out of sight and out of mind.

Last year I threw the brightly colored hand-painted ornaments away. It was a drastic action, but one I considered necessary because every year while getting my other decorations out, their diminished brightness reduced the joy of my Christmas preparations.

I though by getting rid of the ornaments I would finally be free from the emotional pain that endured because of that lost friendship. But I was wrong. This year, when I realized the ornaments were gone, the empty feelings remained.

I know how to put away decorations. I pack them neatly in boxes to store on a shelf or under the basement stairs. But I've never learned where love should go when it's gone.

✤ A Call In The Night ✤

All parents of teens dread receiving a phone call in the middle of the night.

One middle of the night, just past 1:00 a.m., our phone was ringing.

Our two sons, Maury and Mickey, as well as their two friends, Chris Glaser and Dana Rasic, had been in a serious auto accident.

My husband John answered the phone. Before he hung up, I was almost dressed. He didn't have to tell me. I knew.

The accident happened at the intersection of Highway 24 and Elbert Highway. As we drove out of Calhan and over the hill, I heard John say, "Oh my God!"

The crash sight was about fifteen miles distant, yet he had already spotted flashing lights illuminating the hazy sky.

At the scene, the flashing of those same lights created a surreal atmosphere and numbed our senses.

Was this real, or was it a nightmare?

It was in fact a real nightmare!

The kids had been caravaning home from Colorado Springs as a group. The two carloads of teenagers that followed my son's car witnessed the crash. We were greeted at the scene by these young men who told us the driver of the other vehicle was drunk, but everyone was alive.

We glanced at the demolished vehicles, but our concern was for our sons and their friends. Where were they?

Frantically we went from one ambulance to another, searching until all four were located.

❧❧

Time had little meaning that night in the emergency room. Everything that went on is a permanent blur etched in my memory.

My husband and I, and Chris and Dana's parents, were surrounded and supported by the caring concern of the two carloads of teens, the friends of all of our sons.

As we began to put bits and pieces of information together, we learned some of those teens helped by directing traffic. Others went to make phone calls. It was a cold night; but that didn't stop some of those kids from literally taking the shirts off their backs to control the bleeding of their injured buddies. All of them assumed important tasks and were courageous heroes who made a difference.

⫍⫎

Chris underwent surgery for his dislocated hip and a plastic surgeon stitched his face. He also broke his left wrist.

Dana bumped his head and re-injured a knee that had been previously hurt playing football. Now, future surgery awaits, after the swelling subsides.

In the emergency room, John and I watched the plastic surgeon tediously stitch on Maury and Mickey's faces.

Finally, when it was 8:00 a.m. and light outside, we left the hospital. Maury, Mickey and Dana were released. Chris remained.

⫍⫎

The accident occurred around twelve-thirty a.m. on October twelfth. Mickey's fifteenth birthday. Instead of the turkey dinner he had requested for his birthday meal, we ate pizza, drank milk shakes, and celebrated life.

❦ The Champion ❧

As I looked at the crowd gathered in Calhan's gym, I saw folks from many neighboring communities flocked together to witness what they hoped would be an exciting boys basketball game between the hosting Bulldogs and the Peyton Panthers. They were not disappointed.

At the end of first quarter play, the score was tied at 17. When the half-time buzzer sounded, Peyton was on top by three, with the score 34-31. Calhan played catch-up when they returned to the court for the second half, and by the end of the third quarter had worked their way to a 3 point, 49-46 lead.

The players on both teams desired to be the champion of the contest and an intense fourth quarter followed. When time on the clock ran out, Calhan had won, 73-64, but it had been a dogfight to the very end.

The eyes of most in the gym that night were riveted to the action on the court, thinking that was where the victorious champion would be determined. Even though my son plays on Calhan's team, my eyes occasionally drifted to Jan Eggleston, the mother of three Peyton players — son Bryan Rizuto, and daughters Kathy Rizuto and Nori Eggleston. Jan's presence was a testimony of dedicated love and support.

When I met Jan several years ago, she and her husband Lyman, a Denver-based airline pilot, had just settled in the Peyton community. They were intent on building their separate families into one cohesive and supportive unit.

I'm sure life had trials as this group of sibling rivals strived to live under one roof, but because love was in abundance, it worked.

The family bond was intact when the veritable bolt of adversity struck. Jan was ill. Multiple Sclerosis the diagnosis.

During the course of her illness, I witnessed and admired Jan's spunky spirit. Through it all she kept a bright smile and a positive outlook, even when the looming horizon appeared bleak and foreboding.

As Jan's symptoms intensified, she had to endure the limitations her illness imposed on her independence. With dignity and grace she accepted using a cane, then a walker, and finally -- a wheelchair.

When school started this past fall, a difficult decision had to be made. With the children gone all day to school, when Lyman was flying, nobody would be available to help Jan attend to basic body needs and functions. It became necessary for Jan to move away from her home, husband and children -- and into a nursing home in Colorado Springs. The move, an incredibly unselfish gift of love, allowed her children the necessary freedom to fully participate in school activities. Separated from her family, it became increasingly complicated for Jan to remain actively attuned to her children's lives and interests.

It was cold the night Jan was wheeled into the gym to watch her children play basketball. Lyman's devotion to his wife was evident as he took off her coat. Working a zipper and getting her arms out of the sleeves was beyond Jan's capabilities.

When son Brian scored a bucket, even though his mother could not move her arms to bring her hands together in applause, I witnessed pride beaming on her face and knew she was cheering in her heart.

All the athletes on the court that night had worked hard to develop their physical abilities to maximum potential. Each player wanted to be a factor in capturing a victory so their team could be proclaimed the champions of the contest. But quietly, just inside the door was a dedicated mother supporting her children from the confines of a wheel chair. Because of her abiding love and enduring spirit, in spite of physical struggle and adversity, I proclaim her Champion.

❧ *Looking Back On Happy Memories* ❧

I recently went through my 'baby pictures' purposely trying to recall what I was thinking of or feeling at the moment each childhood photo had been taken. It's good to occasionally get out the boxes and books of old family pictures and take a break from the busyness of day-to-day routine.

There is one picture of me with my brother and sister that I don't like. I can't remember any details, but obviously, for some reason, I was upset and had been crying. When I get to the page where it appears, I quickly turn on to the next.

Leafing further into the album, there's a Christmas picture of all the cousins. I'm in the front row, probably eight-years-old, and flanked on both sides by two younger cousins who I perceive looked up to me as a role model.

Eventually I'm past my childhood and on to pictures of John and me as newlyweds. In the earliest photos, members of his family or mine were included. Before much time passed, however, it became apparent a new independent family was emerging. First one son, Maury; then another, Mickey, became a featured and important part of this new family unit.

There are pictures quickly snapped while doing dishes or painting the house, representing ordinary daily life. The progress of a lengthy remodeling project is portrayed in others. Some show little boys enjoying an evening bath together. Then suddenly, those same little boys seem to become young men playing ball, or formally dressed for the prom with a special friend at their side.

In the frenzy of domestic routine, the things that *have* to be done usually get done. The beds are made. The floor is swept. The furniture dusted. The meals cooked. The bathroom cleaned. The clothes washed and pressed. Day by day the necessary chores are accomplished and lives are lived.

I heard myself say, "Oh, I remember this day at the zoo . . . Look at this picture of the boys sitting on the kitchen table licking cookie dough off the beaters . . ." Over and over these stirred up memories ended with a phrase like, " . . . and I remember it was such a fun day!"

While looking at pictures of the ordinary, I realized I had been blessed with an abundance of good times. What a shame I was too busy doing all those things that *had* to be done to be cognizant of my joy and happiness.

❧ *Life Isn't Always Fair* ❧

*S*unday morning I stepped off an elevator seeking the office of the hospital's executive director. Maury, our eighteen-year-old son, had been admitted to the hospital ten days earlier with mononucleosis. Because of irregularities in his care, my present quest was to deliver a letter recounting doctor negligence. I didn't expect the administrative offices to be open on the weekend. I just wanted to slip the envelope under the door, confident it had reached its intended destination.

Just as I started down the hall, the door to another elevator opened and out stepped a casually dressed man.

"Sir, there's a woman looking for you," said the janitor who had helped me find my way.

Realizing this man was the hospital administrator, I turned to greet him. I felt fortunate to personally hand-deliver my letter, along with a brief explanation about why it had been written. He seemed a warm and caring person, genuinely concerned about the events that had gone on within 'his' hospital one week earlier.

☙❧

My husband John, our sixteen-year-old son Mickey, and I arrived at the hospital early that prior Sunday morning. Maury's condition had improved since his admission to the facility, so we were caught off guard when a serious-faced nurse met us as we walked down the hall.

"Your son's temperature went up last night," said the nurse. "We put a call in to the doctor and he prescribed something for the fever. We expect the doctor to be in to see your son shortly."

I was glad the nurse told us of Maury's condition before we entered his room. Her warning allowed us to mask our mounting concern. Typically a person with 'mono' isn't hospitalized, but Maury's swollen tonsils were minimizing his airway.

Throughout the morning we listened to Maury's labored breathing, while patiently waiting for his doctor to arrive.

Finally, when it was nearing noon, my son, who one week

earlier had played varsity basketball, asked, "Mom, isn't there a machine that can help me breath?"

My worry immediately turned to panic.

Throughout the next several hours we helplessly watched while waiting for Maury's doctor to arrive. The nurses placed frequent calls to the doctor's answering service. Calls that went unanswered. As our concern intensified, we asked for our son to be seen by another doctor. *Any* other doctor.

We were told another doctor, due to professional ethics, would not step in unless Maury stopped breathing or his doctor ordered a consultation.

We had become powerless prisoners, locked into a protocol that seemed to protect the 'brotherhood of physicians' rather than the patient.

Finally, at three-thirty that afternoon, Maury's doctor arrived. Consultations with specialists were ordered. Maury was whisked off to the Cardiac Intensive Care Unit, where intravenous drugs were administered to reduce his inflamed and swollen tonsils. A surgeon was in the hospital and standing by. A tracheotomy would be performed if there was no improvement in Maury's condition within one hour.

As the hour passed, the medication worked and the surgery became unnecessary. Even though air flowed in and out of Maury's lungs with greater ease, his anxiety remained. For he had witnessed, and couldn't easily forget, how powerless we had been in confronting the 'system' to secure the medical help he had so desperately needed.

In the comparative calm that followed this nightmarish day, one of the consulting specialists took a dramatic, unusual stand and agreed to take over Maury's care. We felt no joy, only relief, as we officially changed doctors.

అలిఐ

Our doorbell rang late the evening before Calhan's team was to make their first appearance in the district basketball tournament.

Maury, who had come home from the hospital three days earlier, appeared so tall and thin as he answered the door. The physical stress of fighting illness had melted over thirty pounds from his body.

After welcoming his visiting teammate, Maury went to his room and returned carrying his basketball uniform.

"These shorts should fit you better than the ones you've been wearing," Maury said with a chuckle. After a verbal exchange of sincere good wishes, the door closed, blatantly shredding the last lingering remnant of tattered and torn hope. Unknowingly, Maury had already played his final high school basketball game. The opportunity to ever dribble, pass and shoot a basketball in a state tournament game would be a reality for his teammates -- but not for him.

My eyes filled with tears as I watched my son leave the living room in search of solitude. My heart ached because I knew one of Maury's childhood dreams had been shattered by the tough luck of ill-timed bad health. The fact that life isn't always fair is a hard lesson to learn. Even so, I knew this strong, broad-shouldered young man would, in private, find the strength to pick up and make the most of the remaining splintered fragments of his senior year.

The sun would rise upon better and brighter tomorrows.

❧ *Mom* ❧

ecause it was nearing bedtime, the four-year-old girl climbed up into the big rocking chair and onto Dad's lap. She had always felt safe, secure and protected when surrounded by his strong yet loving arms. With wide-eyed innocence, she precociously looked up to Dad and asked, "Is Mom going to be okay?"

Dad wanted to offer total reassurance, but couldn't. Instead, he fought back tears and tightly held his child close.

❧❧

A family, children of their own to nurture and love, had been a shared desire of this man and his wife. With the help of University Hospital physicians, their dream became reality. They became Mom and Dad when they were blessed with two 'miracle' children -- first a son, and three years later, a daughter.

Then came Mom's cancer.

If anyone ever faced cancer with a positive attitude, Mom did. She made the necessary choices about treatment, but always with Dad by her side providing unwavering support.

Even though the children were only four and seven, Mom and Dad agreed to be open and honest when discussing Mom's cancer with them. In all good conscience, they couldn't tell the children, "Don't worry. Everything is going to be okay." They couldn't do that because they didn't know that.

Instead, they told the children, "Mom is gong to take medicine and it's going to make her very sick; but it will also help in the long run."

Mom didn't want to leave her family while having chemotherapy so she chose to stay at home and travel back and forth to the hospital as an outpatient. Mom got sick, lost her hair, and underwent numerous surgical procedures. Sometimes she continued to function only because of her family.

Together they discovered it's the little things, the everyday things, that really matter. Family, friends, and relationships became increasingly important. That's not to say they didn't nitpick, because they did. But their appreciation and love for one another grew.

∽∽

These difficult years were also rich -- full of living, laughing and loving. Mom enjoyed family activities, but learned she must pace herself, allowing time to rest. She enjoyed time to watch the changing of the seasons and the vitality of nature visible from her window seat. Because of Mom's intimacy and communion with nature, she wrote beautiful poetry.

One Autumn day the family drove to the mountains. While eating lunch in Marble, Colorado, they heard that several years previously a train had turned over, scattering pieces of pure white marble near the track. Because it was snowing and the air was brisk, Mom watched from the car while Dad and the children went to search for bits and pieces of beautiful white rocks. In addition to many small chunks, they scavenged one large piece of marble. With all the strength they could muster, their souvenir of a memorable day together was loaded into their car and taken home.

Once home and unloaded, the large white marble rock was placed in a focal location and surrounded by the smaller ones. A few days later Mom said, "I wish you'd lay that large piece of marble down so it doesn't look so much like a tombstone."

∽∽

Ultimately, after six years of various cancer treatments, Mom's doctors said, "There's nothing more we can do."

Because mom possessed a spunky spirit, she and Grandma traveled to the Bahamas for treatment not available in the United States. In a warm and tropical paradise, as sun kissed the beautiful sandy beaches, their skin became tan. Mom grew better and stronger. After many weeks of treatment, she and Grandma returned home.

∽∽

Within one year, any lingering rays of glimmering hope had faded and the horizon was bleak and dark. Once again, Mom's condition had deteriorated and another trip to the Bahamas was scheduled.

Mom cried before she left; but her tears were not for herself. Mom wept because she knew pain and tough times were ahead for her family. That was the last time Dad ever saw Mom cry.

∾★

One last family vacation was planned.

Dad and the kids were going to join Mom and Grandma for a tropical 'spring break' holiday. Then, together, they would bring Mom home.

It had seemed a good idea, but the reality was harsh and cruel.

No one had to tell the children, now eleven and fourteen, that Mom was in serious trouble. They could see it.

Dad wanted to immediately pack up and bring Mom home. Resisting, she said, "No. I can make it. The kids have some rough times ahead. I want them to have a good time."

In her weakened and rapidly deteriorating condition, Mom wasn't able to join her family as they swam in the ocean, enjoyed the beach, and discovered the island's beauty. But she could sit by the swimming pool and watch them splash and play together.

During a sleepless tropical night, Dad was up, walking about the apartment. Light from the courtyard filtered in and illuminated the form of his son, who, instead of sleeping, was earnestly in prayer.

After those few days of basking together in the warmth that radiated from this final holiday, the family boarded a plane and returned home.

∾★

Mom wasn't home long. Only three days. The return flight had been on a Thursday. The following Monday Mom was admitted to the hospital.

In frustration, during this time of helpless watching and waiting, the son asked Dad, "Can't they cut the cancer out?"

"No," Dad replied. "It's past that."

After sharing a good cry, the son quietly said, "I prayed God would take Mom's pain away -- and now He's going to."

Mom died that Thursday.

∾★

Because of Mom's giving nature, her children learned to be aware of the needs of others and to love unconditionally.

Because of Mom's example, her children learned to live life to the fullest -- unafraid of the unknown.

Because of Mom's intimate communion with nature, her

children learned to appreciate the beauty of the out-of-doors. They witnessed its vital ability to create and restore.

Because, even in the end, Mom allowed time for recreation, her children learned the importance of taking time to live, laugh, and love.

Though the time Mom was allotted to spend with her 'miracle' children was short, she successfully taught them by example. The strength of her faith will continue to light up their lives and they will never walk alone.

The essence of Mom's character will live forever, enshrined in the hearts of all who know her.

⚬⚬⚬

A grassy, windswept hill with the grandeur of Pikes Peak visible in the distance is Mom's final resting place. There's no large monument or stone marking the grave. Her children had their own beautiful idea for an appropriate monumental tribute.

Using several small pieces of pure white marble, collected on a family outing, they inscribed the ground with the simple three-letter word synonymous with undying love.

✑ *Memories* ✑

*I*mmediately after the ceremony, the custodial staff was busy putting up the chairs. Graduation was over and it was time to clear out and clean up the gym.

Several hours later, after all our guests had gone home and the celebration was over, I washed the final pot and put away the now empty platters. I was tired, yet unable to sleep. Restless, I settled in the recliner and put my feet up to relax and unwind.

It had been a monumental, happy, yet emotional day. Maury, my first-born son, had become a high school graduate, eager for life's awaiting adventures.

At the various banquets and events preceding this climactic day, I heard, "You have completed your *formal* education and are now ready to begin your *practical* education," said to the graduates numerous times in various ways. That was what I thought about on graduation night.

Completing assignments, studying, and passing tests have been routine activities during Maury's past several years. The path leading to the future is visible for only a short distance before it becomes obscured from sight by a rising bend. The school of life and hard knocks has officially arrived for my son.

As a typical loving mother, I tried to protect both of my children by attempting to keep them safe and free from physical harm and emotional pain. I am also intensely aware this lofty desire is impossible to accomplish. Even during childhood's *formal* education, life and its lessons in *practical* education are all too frequent and familiar.

Maury adapted to the various personalities of teachers and classmates. If assignments were not in on time or completed according to directions, he learned there would be a penalty to pay.

Athletics taught the value of sportsmanship, fair play, and team work as a method of achieving a common goal. Accomplishing a sweet victory is, and always will be, more palatable than accepting the bitterness of defeat.

In addition to reading, writing, and arithmetic, Maury has already learned by experience of the hurt that can be caused by basic inhumanity, jealousy, and greed.

Every time he looks in the mirror he faces the lingering scars of being victimized by another's irresponsible actions.

He knows life isn't always fair and its lessons are hard and painful.

Because I know these lessons must be learned and relearned over and over again, I cried.

When I finally did go to bed, a restless night followed. Since then, several days of doing routine activities have relieved my tension. The floor has been mopped and is no longer sticky from spilt punch. The leftover food has either been eaten or tucked in the freezer.

My oldest son has graduated. The party is over and society says my job as 'mother' has essentially been completed. But no matter what life deals my son, my precious memories will always remain -- memories of an innocent, blond-haired little boy climbing up on my lap to surprise me with a fistful of freshly picked dandelions -- and memories of an enlightened young man, standing tall and proud in cap and gown, giving me a beautiful red rose and a hug while whispering, "I love you."

❧ Ladies & Lunches ❧

I recently met my friend Janet for a leisurely lunch at Pizza Hut. For two hours, we were totally occupied just talking and laughing.

"Do you have a quiet corner table?" we asked Paul, our cute and courteous waiter. "One where we can talk?"

Throughout our meal, Paul pampered us. When our glasses were empty, he quickly brought refills. Several times he asked if there was anything more we wanted to order. Our leisurely lunch lasted so long, Paul eventually teased us by asking, "Do you two want to rent or sign a lease?"

A week later, Janet and I indulged in another recreational outing at the same restaurant. Because Paul had proven to be so wonderfully accommodating, we were delighted when he was the waiter who greeted us.

After requesting our same quiet, corner table, Paul quickly took our order and proceeded to provide his typical attentive service.

I didn't think we had been at the restaurant *too* long, when Paul appeared with a big grin and announced, "Well, you've broken your record."

"Have we already been here longer than the last time?" asked Janet.

"Well, you know women," I added apologetically.

"Yeah, I know about women!" said Paul. "I've got a wife *and* a mother!"

"And," I reminded Janet, "Paul doesn't even know we sat in the car out in the parking lot and talked for thirty minutes before we decided to come in and order!"

A bewildered expression crossed Paul's face as he turned to attend to his other customers.

Later Paul asked if we wanted our uneaten pizza reheated or boxed to go. When we decided to divide it and have it put in *two* little boxes to go, Paul just smiled and obliged.

Paul was quick to complete any task Janet and I requested. He even went beyond the expected! It puzzled us when we noticed Paul walking next door to Dairy Queen. When he returned, we were overwhelmed when be carried two dishes of ice cream, for us! What a welcomed and appreciated surprise! With ice cream, Janet and I had been provided with ample reason to stay longer.

A little later, after asking if we needed more pop, a mischievous grin spread across Paul's face. Reaching into his pocket, he pulled out his keys and said, "This key is for the front door, and this one is for the back."

"Are you ready to close?" asked Janet.

"No," Paul said with a chuckle. "Not until eleven."

The next time Paul came to get our empty glasses for a refill, he asked, "What are you two doing? Writing a book?"

When he returned with our pop, he asked, "What chapter are you on?"

"Twelve," answered Janet.

"I was just checking," said Paul. "I wanted to make sure you were done with the preface."

Over three hours after entering the restaurant, we finally stood at the register to pay our bill. "Remember, I want to read the first copy," quipped Paul as he closed the cash drawer.

When Janet and I responded by giggling, Paul seemed bewildered by our sense of humor. What we knew, and he didn't, was that our encounter would end up in print.

As we pushed the door open to exit, Paul gave our evening an appropriate ending when he cheerfully said, "We open at eleven."

✎ Enlightenment ✎

At our house, we've been arguing about the lights. It's not a new argument. We've always had discussions about how many lights need to be on and how brightly. Recently, however, the frequency has drastically increased.

I prefer soft, indirect table lamps with three-way light bulbs illuminated at their lowest wattage. In contrast, my family thinks the purpose of lights is to be able to *see*.

After a recent light discussion, I went to bed, turned off the lights and in my private world of deep, dark, introspective thought became enlightened. I realized the increased confrontation over the lights was an exterior symptom caused by current change within our family structure. Our oldest son, Maury, is heading off to college. He's leaving home and will be out of my grasp.

To pacify my need for some token semblance of control, I've appointed myself keeper of the lights and claimed all the light switches *mine*! I've become stark raving mad, assumed total authority over each and every light switch throughout our house and driven my family crazy!

❧❧

In the process of growing up, children aren't the only ones developing and experiencing change. Rather, it is a mutual process of ebb and tide for both parent and child. Natural transitions rarely occur smoothly or simultaneously.

There have been times when my son's growth surpassed mine and I was left way behind balking in the wake of the passing furor -- needing more time before I could muster up sufficient balance to venture yet another step into an unknown and previously untraveled journey.

It wasn't very long after I brought my new born babe home from the hospital that he began to push away from me with all his might. I wanted to cuddle and rock. He wanted freedom to discover and explore his new world.

By the time he was five years old, he had his own bike and was ready to take on an ever bigger world. He increasingly sought to expand the boundaries of permissible exploration and adventure. If I gave permission to ride his bike within a two-block radius, he lobbied for the right to travel three blocks from home.

I also recall times when I was willing to take a new step before my child was ready.

When Maury was ten years old, like it or not, to camp he went. Midweek, I got a call from the camp director, who suggested I come get my child. After talking to Maury on the phone and realizing how unhappy he was, I agreed to come and get him that very day.

The next day the mailman delivered a postcard Maury had written and mailed before being rescued from camp. It clearly and simply said:

> Dear Mom and Dad,
>   I don't like camp. I'm homesick. I want to go home.
>   Love Maury

I had been responsible for causing my child this unnecessary misery by forcing him to go to camp and had to come to grips with my pangs of guilt.

ﹰﹰﹰ

My son has left for college. *He's* eager for this next new step. *I'm* not.

For the past eighteen years I've known this day was coming. But, the all-at-once suddenness of its arrival has caught me off balance.

The simple facts are hard to accept. There is one less place to set at the table. His dirty clothes are now his responsibility. I no longer need to sleep lightly until he comes home at night -- and, even when he comes home for the weekend or vacation, *it will never be the same again.*

I need a little more time for all this enlightenment to penetrate the deep darkness of my introspection. Time to see his silver lining shining out from behind my gray cloud. Time to realize some very bright possibilities are waiting ahead.

Allowed time and understanding, I will catch up to my son's desire to press onward and outward to new horizons.

Through this time of high anxiety and transition, so much is beyond my grasp. I need the pacifying security of exercising authority and control over something concrete I can firmly grip. Anything! -- Even if it's just a light switch.

❧ *The Gift Of Love* ❧

Thanksgiving 1988 was a joyous celebration at the Wisconsin country home of Dr. Lester Thompson.

Les, his wife Linda, and their three sons, Kevin, Ricky and Jesse, ages fourteen, twelve and eight, respectively, had invited friends to share their holiday feast. It was a day of good food, conversation, laughter, and shared love. One which, in addition to appeasing hunger, warmed the heart and filled the soul.

The next morning, with the holiday over, life as usual arrived with sunrise. Les began his day by doing chores and feeding livestock before heading off to make his hospital rounds. Sick and hurting patients also began arriving at the general practitioner's office, waiting for their appointed time with the physician.

Even though the clock diligently kept ticking away time, Dr. Les Thompson never arrived at his office. The police were called and a search initiated. In spite of the manhunt, it was sunset before knowledge of the tragic death of the head of their home engulfed Linda and her three sons with a shroud of darkness.

That morning, while traveling down the road, en route from the hospital to the clinic, Dr. Thompson was accidentally shot to instantaneous death by the stray bullet of an unaware hunter. His car slowed and traveled about a half mile before finally going off the road and easing to a stop, hidden from view by wooded terrain. It was late in the day before another hunter happened onto the vehicle and discovered the doctor's tragic and untimely fate.

Les Thompson, forty-eight years old, was an educated man with an ingrained love of nature and an appreciation for simplicity. He and Linda shared a common desire to spend time enjoying the out-of-doors. They built their life together on a foundation deeply rooted in mutual Christian faith.

As friends and extended family gathered to support and grieve with Linda and her sons, all were nourished by deep reservoirs of free-flowing living water and sustained by a peace which passeth understanding.

It was Kevin, age fourteen, who voiced a desire to build his father's coffin. It seemed fitting and appropriate -- consistent with his father's unpretentious lifestyle.

Friends and colleagues of Les Thompson didn't have to ask, "What can I do?" or say, "Please let me know if I can help." Instead, busy schedules were abandoned because of a common desire to serve. Those who rallied to help Kevin with the building of a magnificent tribute were bound together by undying devotion and love.

The project began expediently as light-colored oak, selected for its beauty and strength, was carried into a vacated two-car garage. Soon the whirring sound of the power saw could be heard and sawdust filled the air. The warm and distinguishing characteristics of the oak planks became more evident with each manual stroke of the sandpaper. Soon all splintered roughness had been transformed into a smooth and refined surface. Frustration, anger and grief over this tragic and senseless death were vented as hammers pounded nails into the hard oak.

The large wooden box began to take on its right-angled, rectangular shape. Finally, a simple cross was attached to the inside and outside of the coffin lid, providing the only adornment. A well-worn heirloom quilt, which had been in the family for several generations, lined the wooden box, enhancing its intrinsic and natural beauty. This gift of love was now complete.

Following a service celebrating life, the hand-crafted wooden box was buried deep in the bosom of the earth. In addition to the mortal remains of Dr. Lester Thompson, it contained mementos. Artifacts obtained when he worked among the Navajo Indians were enclosed. So were tokens of love from each of his sons -- like the picture of a rabbit Ricky had given to his father on his last birthday. The simple, hand-crafted oak coffin was a beautiful gift of expressed Christian love and its memory lives on, bringing a warm and glowing light to the dark recesses of heavy hearts.

Linda, now a thirty-eight-year-old widow, will travel with her three sons through the valley of the shadow of death to Colorado, to share aching hearts, tears and Christmas with her parents, Reverend Bob and Esther Fortenbaugh. Together they will experience the inextinguishable joy of Christmas.

✑ Weeping Willow ☙

When we first moved to Calhan, we lived in a small rental house. During that first year we enjoyed the community and decided to investigate the possibility of buying a home. After looking at several houses on the market, we took the big plunge and made our purchase.

It was springtime when we moved in, so, after getting settled, my husband's attention drifted outside. One of the first times John mowed the lawn, something got caught in the mower. After the engine stopped, he got down on his hands and knees to investigate.

"What is it?" I asked.

"You know," he replied, "I think I've found a willow tree trying to grow. I'm going to pound a stake here so I'll stop mowing it off and give it a chance."

Sure enough, once allowed, it grew vigorously and the small seedling proved itself to be in fact a willow. Now, seventeen years have passed and that sprout has become an enormous tree -- much taller than the house!

In the summer, the weeping willow's graceful branches bow down, touching the grass. And, when the lawn is mowed, it still gets caught up and tangled in the mower.

It's incredible that what began as something so small and unnoticeable could grow to become so dominant and overpowering.

Ted Bundy said that's what happened to him.

In a pre-execution interview with Dr. James Dobson, Bundy said he was raised in a good home by loving parents. Yet, early in adolescence, he, just like many other boys, began to leaf through the magazines available at numerous retail outlets -- magazines which featured photos of partially dressed, exposed women. Those pictures whetted a thirst that ultimately became unquenchable. What began as a sampling grew into a monstrous appetite, desiring more, and more, and more.

Addiction to hard-core pornography and 'slasher' film was what Bundy said ultimately drove him to act out fantasies and triggered his hideous and repugnant crimes of rape and murder.

Many experts reject Bundy's pornography addiction theory.

They say pornography may be a contributing stimulus to sex-related murders, but not the strongest, most compelling factor.

Ted Bundy is dead. As a penalty for his ugly, violent crimes, he was executed in Florida's electric chair. Though Ted Bundy is dead, unanswered and troubling questions remain.

I've thought a lot about Bundy.

I've thought about how he filled his mind with ugly visions.

I've thought about how those visions grew until they, like the willow tree, became dominant and overpowering.

I've thought about the awfulness of his crimes and wondered if he ever felt remorse.

I've wondered if he ever wept.

Finally brothers and sisters, keep your thoughts on whatever is right or deserves praise: things that are true, honorable, fair, pure, acceptable, or commendable.

Philippians 4:8   (GODS WORD)

I'm going to try not to think about Ted Bundy anymore.

ᘛ Radiating Love ᘚ

Visits with my ninety-three-year-old Grandma Eva became poignant and bittersweet. Because I loved her, being together was always sweet. Saying good-by became bitter because parting hurt. It hurt with a heartfelt piercing pain, caused by the realistic knowledge *any* visit might be the *last* visit.

Grandma Eve was fortunate. Though her health declined and her vision was limited, with the assistance of nearby family she was always able to live at home. Her lifelong determination and self-reliance provided a personal role model. I have Grandma to thank for the inherently independent nature passed on to me through my mother.

Much of Grandma's youth was spent on the untamed, expansive eastern Colorado prairie surrounding her father's homestead, near Kirk. She and Granddad Ora were schoolmates and neighbors. As a young seventeen or eighteen year old woman, Grandma returned to New York to live with her mother. But, just like a Cinderella story, Granddad Ora missed the only woman he would ever love and took off after her.

Grandma listened to her heart, instead of her mother, and the pair were married, June 29, 1914. Together, they returned to Colorado, homesteaded and built a life they were destined to share for sixty-two years -- until Granddad Ora, age eighty-three, died in 1976.

Grandma Eva was a lady unimpressed with the grand and glorious. She preferred simplicity. In January 1983, she was thrilled when I sent her a box of pinto beans. Her written response was, *"No one would have ever thought of me with something to eat like you have, and I love you dearly. I'm cooking beans today and happen to have some bacon on hand to season them. They are about the nicest and cleanest I've ever seen . . . Thanks for thinking of me and taking time to wrap them and everything, as I know you are busy. I do love you all."* Then, because she never intended for anyone to go out of their way for her, she added, *"PS Don't send anything more, as postage is too high."*

Grandma Eva chose a life tied to the land she and Granddad tamed, tilled, and loved. Yet, she vicariously enjoyed hearing all about the adventures of her children and grandchildren. When a great-granddaughter went on a 1986 trip to New York, Grandma wrote and expressed a rare regret. *"Stacey has been so good to write me* and sent me a card of the Statue of Liberty . . . I told her I had seen it when I was a child, and wanted to go up in it, but Father said, "NO!" - - I have always wished I had gone up in the Statue of Liberty."

Though Grandma's youthful and sprightly, high-steppin' style ultimately became weary and replaced with slow, small shuffling steps, she didn't complain. Rather than bemoan the situation, she addressed her plight with humor. In a 1986 letter she wrote, ". . . so gave up and went to the Doctor, as I just about could not walk, and my hands and wrists were so bad I could hardly use them. Well, he gave me high hopes by telling me I will always have it, and found a million other things wrong, and gave me pills instead of candy . . . Stay young, as old age isn't funny."

There comes a moment when a dying person needs death, just as a sleepy person needs sleep. For my Grandma Eva, that moment came in the evening of February 2, 1989.

Her funeral was held the following Monday. Dressing for the occasion, I started to put on a dark-colored suit; then changed my mind. Instead of something drab and dreary, I decided to wear dusty pink. For, I wasn't going to Grandma's funeral to grieve her death. I was going to participate in a celebration of her life.

Family and friends gathered at the little church in Kirk, braving the cold blast of arctic weather, to pay a final tribute. Though most of Grandma Eva's lifelong friends preceded her in death, one of the ladies in attendance had been her close friend since 1907.

While listening to the service, I realized, though everyone gathered was paying respect to the same person, each had very different and personal memories. I remembered stopping at my grandparents' house in November 1966, to tell them my Dad had died during open-heart surgery. At some point, I realized Granddad and Grandma weren't in the living room with us. Concerned, I went to search for them and make sure they were all right. When I found them, they were back in their little laundry room. They were alone, embracing, and supporting one another. Only I have that memory.

Thanksgiving Day was Grandma Eva's final visit to my home. During that afternoon, Mom made a point to take a picture of Grandma and me, together. For the picture, Grandma reached out to me with her warm, loving hand and smiled, looking at me through eyes that twinkled as if she could vividly see.

After the funeral service, I filed past her casket and paused. This time I extended my hand to hers. Though her hand was cold and lifeless, I felt the radiating warmth of her love. —I always will.

⋞ *Pictures* ⋟

W hen I saw the return address, I tore the envelope
open, eager to know its contents.

Though I didn't meet Tressie at my grandmother's
funeral, I saw her there and became aware of the special relationship
the pair had enjoyed. She had known my Grandma Eva much
longer, and in a very different way, than I had. They shared an
enduring friendship that remained constant and intact since 1907.

Because I wanted to get to know Tressie, I wrote to her. Tressie's
quick reply to my letter gave hope that she, too, might like to know me.

"I adored your Grandmother," Tressie wrote in the letter. "We
laughed and enjoyed our times together. I could tell you many
things about her early life and of growing up on a dry land fam . . . I
would love to know you better, and to have you come to see me. I
am sure Eva would be pleased if we became friends."

I was elated. I wanted to visit this special lady to hear her stories.
Yet, simultaneously, I felt a frustrating sense of urgency. After all, I was
fully aware a visit with Grandma Eva, no matter how desperately
desired, was now too late and impossible. Tressie, too, was up in years.
Visiting her was an opportunity that, likewise, could just pass away.

In spite of desire, the time simply wasn't there. Looking at my
calendar, the dates were committed with things that had to be done
before my husband and I left to spend a week in California. It wasn't
possible to accommodate a minimum six-hour block of time to drive
to Tressie's home in Stratton. My visit would have to be postponed.

❧◦❧

Pictures! Everywhere I looked, people were taking pictures.
Pictures with Mickey Mouse. Pictures in front of Sleeping Beauty's
castle. In Disneyland, everyone seemed to be taking pictures. Even
pictures of people taking pictures!

I became so aware of people and cameras, that during my recent
trip to California, I realized I must have been in hundreds of
pictures. Pictures that would help other people recall their special
times. Pictures that would become treasured keepsakes in their

photo albums. And, even though my image could appear in many, they were pictures I would never see.

∂∾⤵

Once back home, only a couple of days passed before I picked up the phone and called Tressie. With a free day before me, I was eager to make her acquaintance.

When Tressie answered the phone, I learned she had accidentally fallen down the previous day and suffered a broken wrist. Now, arm in a cast, she was staying pretty close to her ice pack and easy chair. She was pleased at the prospect of a visitor to help pass the time.

Early that same afternoon, I found myself at Tressie's door. After greeting her with an affectionate hug, we settled ourselves for conversation.

I had taken along my family album. It included pictures of my children with Grandma Eva and Granddad Ora. After Tressie and I looked at my pictures, we looked at hers. During our afternoon together, Tressie and I shared laughter, memories, love and tears.

I had expected Tressie's pictures to include ones of her late husband and their children and grandchildren. I wasn't surprised her collection also included several of my grandparents. Together, as we continued looking through her pictures, one suddenly caught my attention. It was familiar. Too familiar. It was of me!

As I held it close for inspection, Tressie said, "Your grandmother sent that one to me after she and Ora celebrated their sixtieth wedding anniversary."

"Yes, I remember the day," I said as I continued to study the photo. "This is me, and here's my husband John," I said as I pointed to the likeness of how we looked fifteen years earlier. "Granddad is holding my youngest son, Mickey," I continued. "And this is Maury, standing by Grandma."

It was a shocking surprise. There, in the home of a lady I had never before met, I saw a picture of me and my family I had never before seen.

∂∾⤵

Before the day was over, I took a picture of Tressie. I wanted the photo, not only because she helped me focus on a clearer and sharper perception of my Grandma Eva, but to help me remember Tressie and the special time she and I shared. Tressie's picture belongs in my home, in my album.

❧ Cheerful Greetings ❧

Even though it was my day off from work, I intended to get a lot of work done at home. I actually jumped out of bed and immediately wrote a list of chores so I could enjoy a sense of accomplishment each time I crossed off a completed task.

Everything went according to plan until mid-afternoon. I was just finishing the ironing when I heard a sort of humming noise coming from the yard. Hurrying to look out the window, I caught sight of a hummingbird drinking from the feeder I had placed outside on the back deck several days earlier.

Almost breathlessly I stood watching and listening through our screened back door. Finally the hummingbird perched itself on a high branch of our purple plum tree and seemed to beckon me to come closer and get acquainted.

Ever so carefully and quietly I crept outside. After tiptoeing across our wooden deck, I settled in a chair. While keeping my silent vigil, a second hummer swooped, seemingly out of nowhere, circled the yard and came in for a drink.

The two tiny creatures flitted about our back yard throughout the warm but cloudy afternoon. Each time they paused to sip my home-brewed nectar they reaffirmed their pleasure in the provided refreshment.

The interactions between the birds led me to believe this tiny pair were more than friends. Though less than four inches long, I decided the bigger green bird with a bright red throat must be the male because of his obvious demonstrative behavior. The female, though not quite as large or colorful, was irresistibly decked out in iridescent auburn feathers that glowed in the sunshine like burning embers.

The duo acted as if I wasn't present. Because I didn't want to startle of alarm them, I was afraid to move. Eventually the pair flew off in merry chase, providing me the opportunity to get my camera.

Before I knew it, three hours had flown by. My housework wasn't done. My husband was home from work. Suddenly it was supper time! Where, oh where, had my afternoon gone?

As my husband approached, I gestured for him to walk slowly and quietly. After pointing out one of the birds, again perched high in the purple plum tree, John joined me in my bird watching.

When I whistled, one feathered friend chirped a reply then attentively tilted its head to listen.

Now John, who was avidly watching the hummingbirds, extended a greeting, saying, "Hello, little birds." Then, with a slightly embarrassed look on his face, he turned to me and asked, "What am I doing talking to birds?"

❧❧

Early the following morning as the first rays of sunshine filtered into our bedroom, the humming wing movements of my feathered friends awoke us from a peaceful sleep.

Once again my husband talked to the birds.

This time his greeting *wasn't* cheerful!

October's Story

ach day is shorter. Giant pumpkins are round and ripe. Squirrels busily gather a supply of nourishment to tide them through the coming colder weather. The breeze has become as crisp as the leaves that have fallen from the trees that tower high overhead. Now only a couple of leaves remain, clinging to barren branches.

It was this familiar October panorama that brought Bessie and Lena to mind.

Lena was a slight older lady with fair skin, silver-white hair, twinkling eyes, and a gentle manner. Lena also was a widow.

Bessie, the same age as Lena, had gray hair, large features, skin that still bore the subtle scars of teenage acne, a hearty laugh, and a kind but demonstrative manner. In addition, Bessie had a husband, Joe.

Joe went to play checkers every evening with his friend Stanley. Thanks to the checker games, Bessie and Lena were free to spend time together. After all, Bessie and Lena had been the best of friends since childhood -- nearly eighty years ago.

Late one October afternoon, Bessie and Lena decided to go for a walk. As the pair slowly ventured on their way, the warm sun kissed their glowing faces, even though there was an unmistakable chill to the breeze that blew the brittle fallen leaves. Before long this pair, who had come to lean and depend upon one another for moral and physical support, had traveled to the grassy, tree-covered hill near the edge of town. The hill served as the final resting place for all the good folk who, through the years, had called this community home.

Some people are frightened in cemeteries, especially during October evenings when long, ominous shadows forebodingly accompany one along the way, past the headstones marking the final resting place of the town's dear departed citizens.

But the spirits Bessie and Lena met as they trudged along the overgrown path were friendly. After all, who could possibly fear their favorite schoolmarm. Pausing, they fondly remembered Miss Brooks. When Miss Brooks was Bessie and Lena's first grade teacher, she married and became Mrs. Adams. It was during the third grade that their teacher suddenly died, leaving behind a handsome husband, who, almost overnight, became old and wrinkled. He never did remarry.

Soon the duo came upon Sally's marker. Sally had moved to this small community when Bessie and Lena were in their early teens. Eagerly they had welcomed her as a friend. And, for a few brief years, their duet became a glorious trio, blending the three of them together with a perfect harmony. It was an epidemic of diphtheria that had claimed this dear friend so many long years ago.

Dr. Higbee's headstone was the next to capture Bessie and Lena's attention. For years he had been a tender caregiver, providing medical service to the entire region. He was a friend to all because he considered every individual to be more valuable than the contents of their wallet. Payment for his service occasionally was in the form of money; but more often he accepted eggs, milk, or meat as payment in full. Doc, as he was called, always had a pocketful of Black Jack chewing gum. It was a special treat for the boys and girls who visited his office.

Never did Bessie and Lena go to the cemetery without stopping to visit Lloyd, Lena's husband for over fifty years. Though words were never uttered, Bessie wouldn't dream of interrupting the sweet communion she sensed taking place between Lena and her lover. When Lena was ready to move on, she let Bessie know by simply leading the way.

This pair continued wandering through the cemetery, amid their reveries and memories, until Bessie noticed the breeze had suddenly lost its gentleness and the sun was about to sink behind the horizon. After buttoning their coats, they tied their scarves and started back to town. Silently the duo trudged along, still basking in the warm afterglow of their visit to that quiet hill at the outer edge of town.

It wasn't until they were nearly home that Lena reached out to Bessie, capturing her undivided attention. Then, breaking the silence, Lena said, "You know Bessie, we have more friends buried out on that hill than living here in town."

❧ *Cleaning The Clutter* ❧

*O*ccasionally we all have to clean the clutter from those nooks and crannies where stuff seems to pile up and accumulate.

The kitchen counter is the place in our home where everything naturally gathers. Notes from one family member to another, the television's remote control, junk mail, school books, and telephone messages get strewn all over the counter. Every evening I clean this clutter because I can't rest until the counter is cleared.

On rare occasion I clean out the junk drawer. It's a job nobody likes to tackle because the drawer is filled with things that were put there because there was no other place to put them. Unfortunately, after being shuffled through, most of this junk goes right back into the very same drawer.

Recently I took time to clean the clutter from my address book. I've used the same address book since before I was married. Cleaning it was a chore I had never before tackled. Many of the pages in my old address book were totally filled, leaving no room to squeeze in any new entries. Some of the accumulated names, addresses and phone numbers weren't even accurate.

As I began transferring names from my old address book into the new one, I quickly realized how difficult it is to go through and clean this kind of clutter. It's like walking down memory lane, armed with a giant eraser. It's hard to clean out, throw away and eradicate people -- especially ones who at some time were near, dear, and held in high regard.

Most of the names omitted from my new address book were friends who diminished and faded from our lives.

Some attended graduate school with my husband John, or were our neighbors in the married student housing complex. Together we shared many good times and a common poverty level. Now, I can't even remember their children's names, and have absolutely no idea where on earth they live.

A few names belonged to friends from our high school days, who married and moved away without letting us know their new name or address.

I didn't have to get too far through the book's alphabetically ordered pages, however, before I recognized another category of names to be omitted from my new address book. Right away, under 'A', I came across Stone and Elsie Anderson, my husband's maternal grandparents. They happened to be the first of numerous people who have died since I wrote their name in my address book. Many other friends and relatives, on both sides of our family, have likewise died.

Though dear departed friends and family members have passed on, nothing could ever eradicate the love and emotion that accompanies reflection on the good times we shared together. Even without an earthly address or phone number, I talk to some of them all the time.

❧ Just Like Patty's Doll ❧

*P*atty was a captivating delight to her Uncle Alan. She was a beautiful child with a fresh and pure disposition. Her long and shiny blond hair, a striking contrast to her dark and trusting eyes, served as an appropriate frame for her plump and rosy smiling cheeks.

During one Christmas visit, Patty particularly enamored Uncle Alan by taking him by the hand to show him her doll collection. Together the duo laughed as Chatty Cathy talked, cried right along with Tiny Tears, and held their breath while changing Betsy Wetsy's diaper. Blowing bubbles with Baby Bubbles actually made them both laugh aloud. But, when Uncle Alan got down on his hands and knees and crawled along beside her Bouncing Baby doll, Patty doubled over and giggled with glee.

After discovering what each of Patty's dolls could do, Uncle Alan asked, "Of all these special and beautiful dolls, which one is your favorite?"

"Oh, none of the dolls I've shown you is my favorite," Patty incredulously replied. "I don't think you want to see my favorite doll."

"Yes I do," responded Uncle Alan.

"Are you sure? Really sure?" Patty asked, seeking reassurance.

"Of course I do," emphasized Uncle Alan. "I want to see your favorite doll the most of all!"

Out from under her bed, Patty pulled out a little pink suitcase. After carefully opening the small satchel, Patty picked up and lovingly caressed her favorite doll.

This doll, unlike the others she had shown Uncle Alan, was pathetic and shabby. Only one of the dolls' eyes would open, an entire arm was missing, and her hair was matted, messy, and there were bald spots.

Uncle Alan, more than a little surprised his niece could overlook all of the doll's obvious faults and flaws, asked, "Patty, with all of your beautiful dolls, why do you like this one best?"

"Because," replied Patty. "If I don't love her, nobody will."

❧❧

Christmas is a season of joy -- but not for everyone.

During this time of festivity, when everyone is supposed to be happy, anything in our lives that causes pain or unhappiness becomes magnified and exaggerated.

Due to our inherent human nature, we each have had to deal with disappointment, failure, disagreement and loss. Others have let us down, leaving our anxious anticipation vulnerable to becoming unfulfilled expectation. We've let ourselves down and suffered humiliating embarrassment due to our own failures and shortcomings. Everyone doesn't always get along. Sometimes people bicker. Other times, there's outright separation and strife. And who among us hasn't suffered a painful or even debilitating loss?

Strained, broken or lost relationships are a cause of holiday pain. It hurts to spend Christmas Day with a brother you only speak to for your mother's sake. It's difficult to hang an ornament on the Christmas tree if it was given to you several years ago by someone who betrayed you and is no longer a friend.

The challenge of Christmas is to love unconditionally by letting go of past resentment, bitterness and anger. To love unconditionally means initiating reconciliation and accepting others as they are and where they are, in spite of faults.

Christmas was created by unconditional love.

Its illuminating warmth is powerful enough to transform even the pathetic and shabby into something truly beautiful -- just like Patty's doll.

⊷ A Love Story ⊱

His kidneys ceased to function and a maze of tubes and wires ran into and out of a frail body -- feeding, draining and monitoring vital signs.

Though the illness had progressed over a period of years, there had been many good times. When in remission, he had enjoyed family outings and the love of his adoring wife and their two young children.

While sitting in the hospital room watching him labor for breath as he slept, she thought of those good times past. She thought of the good times they had enjoyed during their courtship. A picnic in the mountains. A day at an amusement park. An evening out at a special restaurant. But of all these pleasant reveries, her reflections lingered on their senior prom. What a handsome couple they had been. When he took her in his arms and held her close to his muscular body, she had felt so safe. As if nothing could ever come between them or spoil their happiness.

Looking at him as he lay on the stark white sheet, he seemed so pale and thin. Nearly lifeless. Yet, the potent influence and example of his life remained a mighty force, present even in the face of inevitable death.

Oh how she had loved, did love, and always would love this man she had married. He had been the rock of her life, and the foundation of her existence.

His rest was interrupted by pain. He responded by fretfully thrashing his arms and legs about his bed and against the restraining bed rails.

Immediately she was at his side. The mere sound of her voice restored serenity to his spirit.

With quiet repose, she reflected on the high points of their life together. By taking inventory, she clearly saw that he had been at his best when parenting their children. He had always given them his time, patience, and unconditional love. Their son and daughter would be the crowning glory of his life. She knew he was who had planted seeds in a fertile and nurturing environment, even though he wouldn't live to reap the harvest.

෩෧

In the spring of 1988, Maury needed the reassurance of holding on to my hand. Maury, then eighteen, was very sick and in the hospital. He experienced how frightening it is when every breath is a labored struggle.

At the end of one of those long days, Maury's pleading eyes became brimming with tears as I stood holding onto his bedrail, saying good-bye.

As his hand slowly reached up for mine, he simply said, "Mom, don't go."

Instantly, my plans changed.

෩෧

Through the years, this mother has learned to relish the magic of the everyday moments. And, now that my boys are essentially grown, I know how very special it has been just to have their hand to hold.

Rite Of Passage

*I*t's been several years since our dog, Shasta, died. I was at work at the Pikes Peak Co op when I got the call. Immediately I headed for home, where I was greeted by my two little boys. Tears were streaming down their cheeks as they blubbered an account of how Shasta had gotten run over.

Before I could go back to work, I had to get this situation under control. For out in our garage were six, two-day-old, puppies -- now orphaned, and crying to be fed.

"Boys," I said, "we all feel bad that Shasta is dead, but we don't have time right now to cry. There is work to do. The only thing we can do for Shasta now is feed and care for her puppies."

The three of us hopped in the car and headed for Thomason's Pharmacy to buy doll bottles, so we could take over the task of feeding the puppies. Next, I called a veterinarian, who provided a formula to substitute for Shasta's milk. After brewing this concoction, the boys got busy and I returned to work.

The one thing neither I nor either of the boys could do was pick up Shasta from the side of the road and bury her. That final unpleasant duty was left for my husband John to do when he came home from work.

Life is full of unpleasant duties.

Somebody has to wipe runny noses.

Somebody has to clean up babies after they've dirtied their diapers.

Somebody has to clean up the mess after a sick person vomits all over the carpet.

Somebody has to clean out the yuck that collects in the sink strainer, or that jams up the garbage disposer.

Somebody has to plunge the toilet.

Somebody has to clean out the accumulated moldy food from the containers that hide way in the back of the refrigerator.

Somebody has to empty the kitty box, or use the pooper scooper to clean up the doggie doo.

And, somebody has to bury dead pets after they get run over.

A willingness to do your share of cleaning up messes is a test. It's a test more important than any of the final exams our area graduating seniors will take in the classroom because, taking out the garbage of life is a condition of membership in the adult community.

My youngest son, Mickey, is among this year's graduating seniors. He has grown, matured, and demonstrated a willingness to help clean up life's messes.

Mick is a great cook who can tackle even the most complicated recipes. One day when he was in the middle of baking a coconut cake, the kitchen sink stopped draining. Mick poured in the Drano. Even after an hour of waiting, he continued to see the yucky water still standing, refusing to go on down the drain.

I may be able to wipe runny noses, change dirty diapers, and clean up vomit, but, when I look at putrid water standing in my kitchen sink, I get nauseated.

Mick knew what had to be done and proceeded to do it -- without being asked. All by himself, he went down into the basement, opened the clean-out joint in the sewer line, inserted the drain snake, and went to work. Upstairs, with my stomach wrenching at the thought, I tried to keep from thinking about the accumulated gunk he was catching in the bucket reserved for 'dirty' work.

When the job was completed, Mick came back upstairs. He walked the same, talked the same, and even laughed the same. Yet, I realized that at some point in time, my son had become an adult. He could and would be willing to take out his share of humanity's garbage.

When I sit and watch my son participate in his school's formal graduation ceremony, I'll be witnessing societies 'rite of passage' into adulthood. I'll shed more than one tear for the little boy who, because he has grown and changed, is forever gone. Yet, I'll proudly smile because I know he has become a man.

His shoulders have become broad enough, and his character strong enough, that someday, if the need arises, he'll even be able to gently, tenderly, and lovingly bury a pet.

Ray Of Sunshine

Now that my youngest child has graduated from high school, people have asked me if I'm suffering from the Empty Nest Syndrome.

I usually respond by saying, "I've been too busy to notice." The reality, however, is it's a question I don't know how to answer. Just how does a person feel when they're suffering from this syndrome?

I had Stephen Johnson's Syndrome while I was in college. I had a fever. I broke out with sores from my mouth clear to my stomach. I had to gargle hydrogen peroxide. I remember it took me so long to eat my first meal after returning home from the hospital that my mother thought I should have stayed there a day or two longer.

Yes, I know what the symptoms are for that strange malady, but nobody's told me exactly what to expect or how I'll feel when, and if, the Empty Nest Syndrome should strike. What are the symptoms?

I do know that a couple of days before my son's graduation, I was struck by a dumfounding thought. Suddenly I realized I'm no longer the mother of two children. Instead, I've become the old woman responsible for bringing two college students into being.

To most people this probably doesn't seem shocking -- but for me, it was! This realization hit me so hard, it totally threw my equilibrium off balance. The reason it had such a profound impact is, ever since I was a kid, I separated people whose children were on their own or in college from the rest of the population. It was my arbitrary line dividing *young* people from *old* people.

Suddenly I had to deal with the personal reality that, if both of my sons were in college, I had become indisputably old. In our youth oriented society, being old is a fate about as distasteful as death itself.

When I shared these feelings with several friends at the recent graduation party we hosted for our son, most of them laughed. They made light of the turbulent storm that was rocking my boat.

It was Julie Stjernholm, however, who threw me a lifeline. She provided a much needed ray of sunshine by saying, "Oh Jan, you're not *old*. You've just been *wrong* all these years."

The thought of being wrong made me so very happy! I just hope Julie was *right*!

✑ Bubbles ✑

I was talking on the phone with a friend. I could tell she was happy by the way she was 'bubbling'. Even though I couldn't see her, her pleasure radiated across the miles of phone lines. I was able to sense her free-flowing and animated joy.

When I hung up my phone, I felt better. Because of our conversation, I had become the recipient of a precious gift -- the gift of a day made brighter by her shared happiness.

We've all experienced the exuberance of being so full of personal excitement we could hardly contain our pleasure. We've all felt that inner tumultuous, yet pleasant, urge to 'bubble'.

That telephone conversation with my friend became particularly memorable when, the next time we talked, she apologized for 'bubbling'.

It's exhilarating to share another's bubble of joy. Sharing those 'bubbles' means risking possible rejection; however, usually having our pleasure multiplied, rather than diminished, is the result.

Have you ever watched children blowing bubbles?

You can actually see and hear their pleasure. Young children squeal with delight every time a bubble is blown that's larger than any other. As they chase after small drifting bubbles, their care-free glee is evident. Trying to catch the bubbles before they break is a game.

Look closely at a bubble. The individual colorations and unique designs, floating on its slick surface, become apparent in bright sunlight. Every bubble is different, yet all are illusive and short-lived.

A drifting bubble is a remarkable thing of iridescent beauty -- a fragile, transparent sphere of air, trapped in space; so eager to be free from its filmy container, it's easily burst. A soft landing on grass is sufficient.

Our fragile personal 'bubbles' are just as vulnerable. They, too, can easily be broken; leaving hopes and dreams shattered. Our internal excitement can be carelessly poked and drained by others.

Bubbles come to the top of the water when someone is drowning. The bubbles continue as long as there is breath. When the bubbles cease, so has life.

I've heard someone who is drowning surfaces three times for air I wonder how many times the 'bubbles' of joy, or an adventurous spirit, can be stifled before they cease?

❧ *Balance* ❧

The big black beetle was right in the middle of my path and nearly got squished. I decided I didn't want to look at a yucky spot every time I came around, so I straddled the creature by allowing each of my roller skates to pass by on either side.

Though I hadn't gotten my skates out all summer, I suddenly felt the need to get off by myself for some fresh air and introspective thought. Earlier that day I had transported the belongings of both of my sons to their respective college. Earlier in the week I learned Janet, my good friend and personal confidant was going to move from the area. Obviously, the patterns of my life were about to change. Going to the park to skate seemed like a good way to get away.

Even though the sun had already set, this late August evening was warm. After turning on the tennis court lights, lacing my white leather boots, and fine tuning my FM radio headset, I was ready to roll. It seemed pleasant to get out and move my body while creating a cool breeze as I glided around and around this large cement slab.

While in this subdued mood, I realized I really hadn't gotten outside all summer -- except to take my turn at mowing the lawn. I had allowed most of the summer to pass me by without taking time for play.

Some people think play is an experience reserved for childhood. I believe play to be a necessary ingredient through the course of life.

There are those who would find maintaining an upright posture while roller skating to be work, rather than play. Because it was a favorite activity of my childhood, one I developed by taking lessons for several years, skating for me remains play.

It was in the midst of my play that this big black beetle and I crossed paths.

After rolling past, I made a small circle enabling me to go back for a closer look. After that, on every subsequent lap, I watched for the beetle and observed its progress. Suddenly I realized while I was busy going around in circles, the beetle remained on course, targeting itself in a direct line across the court. Nothing seemed insurmountable or able to alter the beetle's straight-as-an-arrow trek.

After thinking about the beetle's course, I thought about mine.

All summer I had been very much like that beetle. I had engrossed myself in work, both on the job and at home. I hadn't even paused long enough to pick a petunia or savor a sunset. I had merely trekked along on track, almost as if I were wearing blinders that made it impossible for me to see or appreciate my surroundings.

Since meeting up with that big black beetle, I've tried to take some time, every day, to play. Almost every evening, I've paused from my direct course long enough to walk to the park, put on my skates, and go round and around in circles.

It's a matter of maintaining proper balance.

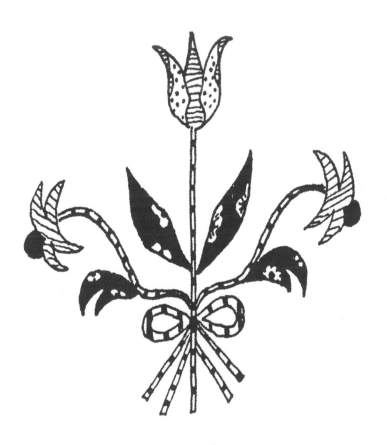

ᢙ Cookies & Milk ᢙ

Mandy, a first grader, had never walked home from school alone. This day would be the first.

Feeling a bit nervous about allowing her daughter to expand her horizons, Mom lectured while Mandy got ready for school. As Mom walked with Mandy to school, she reminded her daughter that the safest course to travel the four blocks back home by herself was to cross the busy street at the light, go two blocks to the grocery store, turn the corner and then walk straight home. Mandy was to look carefully before crossing each street. Mandy wasn't to talk to strangers or dawdle.

With a hug and a kiss, Mandy and Mom parted at the playground fence.

The day was pretty routine and ordinary for both Mandy and Mom. Mandy got a gold foil star on her spelling test and had chocolate milk for lunch.

At home, after making the beds and straightening the house, Mom baked cookies and washed windows. The aroma of freshly baked chocolate chip cookies permeated the entire house, and could even be smelled while she washed the outsides of the windows.

After the final window was washed, Mom noticed it was three o'clock and time for school to get out. With a smile on her face, she put the last pan of cookies into the oven to bake. Mom smiled because it pleased her to realize the cookies would come out of the oven at the same time Mandy should get home. They would be able to take a break together to enjoy warm cookies and a cold glass of milk.

While the cookies baked, Mom went out on the front porch and enjoyed the perfect Indian Summer weather from the vantage point of their glider. Then, as Mom began to see older children whiz by on their bicycles, the timer buzzed. Its signal reminded her to take the cookies from the oven.

After carefully removing the cookies from the cookie sheet, they were placed on a wire rack to cool. Because Mandy still wasn't home, Mom went ahead and rinsed the cookie sheet and made final preparations to start the dishwasher. After putting dishwasher soap in the proper compartments and closing the door, Mom turned the knob and started the appliance.

While attending to all of these routine duties, Mom kept thinking at any moment Mandy would come through the front door and cheerfully exclaim, "Hi, Mom! I'm home." But still, the front door hadn't opened. No greeting had been heralded or heard.

As the dishwasher gurgled and the cookies continued to cool, Mom once again returned to the front porch. Though she looked up and down the street, she could see no Mandy.

Now twenty minutes had passed. Mom knew Mandy should have been able to walk home in half that amount of time. Mom wondered where Mandy could be and worried about what might have happened to her.

Ultimately, another anxious ten minutes would pass before Mandy finally arrived home.

Mom, deciding to allow Mandy to tell her side of the story before passing judgment, asked her daughter for an explanation.

"Well Mom, when I was walking past that vacant lot next to Smith's house, I noticed Sara. She was off of the sidewalk and over under that great big willow tree. Sara was crying because some big boys had taken her doll from her and had thrown it down on the ground. Mom, those boys *broke* Sara's *favorite* doll!"

"I see," said Mom, thinking she understood. "You stopped to help your friend fix her doll."

"Oh! My goodness no!" Mandy incredulously replied, knowing there was no way the doll could be fixed. "I stopped to help Sara cry."

At first Mom was a bit surprised by her daughter's reply. But, after thinking it over, Mom realized Mandy had done a wonderful thing. Mandy had taken time to cry with Sara as an expression of heartfelt sympathy. This six-year-old daughter of hers already knew and understood the ministering power of tears.

After proudly taking Mandy into her arms to welcome her home, they went into the house for cookies and milk. Though the cookies had cooled, they shared the warmth of love.

❧ *Playground Innocence* ❧

*S*arah went to the playground while her mother was nearby practicing with her softball team.

Busy in her pretend sandbox kitchen, she cleaned, baked cookies, and had an imaginary tea party. Sarah's play was not lonely. She had a host of invisible friends to play with.

About twenty minutes later, the opposing softball team arrived at the park. Amy, the daughter of one of these players, also went to the playground to amuse herself. At first, even though both girls were five years old, neither Amy or Sarah talked or interacted. Eventually, Amy's desire to play with Sarah caused her to leave the isolated safety of the swing and move closer.

Sarah responded to the nonchalant overture by asking, "Would you like a cookie?"

As Amy pretended to eat the mud pie confection, the girls exchanged warm smiles. Now, real play could begin.

The afternoon quickly passed. There was no fighting or tears, only giggles and smiles.

Unafraid of possible rejection, Amy innocently asked, "Will you be my friend?"

"Sure," Sarah instantly replied.

❧❧❧

Three ladies and I went out for a snack. While waiting for our order, I casually asked, "How do you guys handle rejection?"

For a time, they incredulously looked back at me, without speaking. I had obviously asked one of those questions nobody expects to be asked. But knowing me, and the fact I'm apt to ask anything, eventually one of them replied, "I don't allow myself to be vulnerable."

"Yeah," agreed the other, "I've learned the hard way. It's really much easier to maintain a distance."

"I choose my friends very carefully," the conversation continued, "because it hurt a lot when one person I did get close to moved away. I won't allow myself to ever get that close to anyone, again."

I had touched a button -- reminding each of relationships that, for some reason, no longer exist. Now, a painful void remains.

෨ඏ

Never have I heard one adult innocently say to another, "Would you be my friend?" No. Adults are much too sophisticated to leave themselves vulnerable to the pain of rejection by so openly exposing a need.

It's much easier to become surrounded with a buffer zone of acquaintances, who move in and out of our lives with little or none of the emotional cost or attachment related to a real and deep friendship.

On the journey from childhood to adulthood, people learn to build isolating emotional walls, regardless of the fact that people *need* people. They always have, and they always will.

I guess I'm a foolhardy slow learner, dreaming the impossible dream, because I naively continue making emotional attachments to the people I care about and interact with.

Yes. I get whammied, fall down, hurt, and bleed -- but, eventually, I've always managed to pick myself up, lick my wounds, and recover.

I consider myself blessed and fortunate because of the joy and pleasure friends have brought into my life. When compared to casual acquaintance, a real friend is rare and precious. Worthy of considerable cost.

My words may differ, but, I hope I'll always possess enough of the innocence of childhood to bravely continue asking, "Will you be my friend?"

❧ *My Honey Doesn't Think It's Funny* ❧

After the three thousand seats in the Broadmoor International Center were filled, women began to sit on the floor, in the aisle, or lean up against the walls around the perimeter of the huge room.

Having arrived an hour early in eager anticipation, I was among the lucky ones with a seat. This day had been marked as a red letter day on my calendar. Barring some major catastrophe, I wouldn't miss hearing Cathy Guisewite, the celebrity speaker at the 5th Annual Women's Life Festival.

Cathy Guisewite is the cartoonist responsible for the 'Cathy' comic strip. Hardly a day goes by when I don't read the newspaper's funny pages. It seems to be a necessary respite from dealing with the harsh realities of real life.

Like all women I know, 'Cathy' struggles with the four basic guilt groups. Food, career, mother, and relationships. Because her frustrations are my frustrations, 'Cathy' often helps me see my life, my circumstances, and my concerns with a touch of humor. Laughing at 'Cathy' is like laughing at myself.

While intently listening to Cathy Guisewite, I began to realize it was hard to tell where Cathy the creator stopped and 'Cathy' the cartoon character started. I was listening to a very funny lady.

When Cathy talked of appeasing uncontrolled late night hunger by squirting whipped cream directly from the aerosol can and into her mouth, I poked my friend and said, "I've done that."

When Cathy talked of balancing her checkbook by simply changing banks and starting over, my friend poked me and said, "I've done that." Then, remembering she was talking to a banker's wife, quickly added, "Of course, that was before we started banking at Farmers State!"

When Cathy talked of eating two-pound bags of M & M's to help vent frustration, every woman in the room entered into a rousing ovation of applause, and my friend and I simultaneously looked at each other and said, "Who hasn't done that?"

Since that day, I've thought about Cathy and her comic strip, and I've thought about me and this weekly column. I've thought about how much I like to try to be funny, and I've thought about how rarely I actually write what I consider to be a funny column. I also thought about how my husband hates it when my writing is funny.

For some reason, if I write about the gross and moldy forgotten food stagnating in the back of my refrigerator, my husband thinks it's a bad reflection on me. If I write about being too uncoordinated to simultaneously walk and chew gum, my husband thinks it's a bad reflection on me. If I write about my hairy legs, big feet, or chubby cheeks, my husband thinks it's a bad reflection on me.

I don't know how many times, after I've written one of my rare but funny columns, I've listened as my perplexed husband asked, "Why do you write bad things about yourself?"

"Don't you think *everybody* has had moldy food in their refrigerator at some time or other?" I reply. Or, "I'm sure I'm not the only uncoordinated person with hairy legs, big feet, and chubby cheeks!"

"But," continues my husband, "I love you! And, because I do, I hate it when you publicly knock yourself."

Unfortunately, that's the way it is with humor. We only laugh at what we can relate to.

❧ Music In The Air ❧

*D*ad couldn't sing. He was tone deaf. He could hear and enjoy music, but his mind couldn't transfer a tone going into his ear into the same pitch coming out of his mouth. Consequently, when I was a child it was fun to coax Dad into singing, and then giggle at his efforts.

Nevertheless, Dad enjoyed music. Anytime the family climbed into the car and headed down the road, it was more apt to be my sister, Mom and me singing that kept us entertained, rather than the radio. We sang simple little rounds and camp songs, as well as Mom's favorite songs, like *Ivory Palaces, Tumblin' Tumbleweeds* or *Deep Purple.* Sometimes we sang in what we thought was glorious three-part harmony.

There was also music in our home. I loved it when Mom played our old upright piano.

My brother Bob, being the oldest, was the first one of us kids Mom chauffeured to and from piano lessons. To say he didn't enjoy them would be an understatement But to this day, Bob still can play his little Indian melody. It was the only piece he ever learned!

Next came my sister. Lois took piano lessons for two or three years and Mom spent those same two or three years reminding her to practice. Eventually Lois stopped taking lessons and Mom made the announcement that if anyone wanted lessons, she would be happy to pay for them, but we would have to ask for them and practice on our own.

I was in the eighth or ninth grade and had played clarinet in the school band for a couple of years before I expressed a desire to take piano lessons. I continued my lessons for about a year. Then, suddenly, I stopped.

Though I've always known why I quit, before now, I've never told anyone. You see, I had taken lessons just long enough for the teacher to tell me it was time to start preparing for my first recital. If taking lessons meant performing in a recital . . . Well, I'd rather *die*! So I quit.

It wasn't playing in front of an audience that bothered me. No. I quit because I was thirteen-years-old and only able to play simple little songs. I also knew that at the recital there would be many little kids, who had taken lessons much longer than I. They would be playing difficult rhapsodies. I was simply embarrassed.

For many years I've longed to own a piano and be able to play it for my own personal release and enjoyment. Once I even bid on a piano at a farm auction -- but someone else bid more.

I did buy a small electronic keyboard and insisted my sons take lessons one summer. But, for me, this scaled down, wired up version of a piano, with several instruments and rhythms, just wasn't the same as owning the real thing.

Recently (oh happy day!) an unexpected opportunity to buy a piano came my way; and jump at it I did!

Now that I have my very own piano, there has once again been music in the air as I've delighted in hunting and pecking at the keys to my heart's content.

After more than a thirty-year pause, I've started taking lessons again. But now I'm older and wiser. The music I make is for *my* enjoyment. When recital time comes around, rather than quit, I'll decline!

❦ Do You Love Me? ❧

"Do you love me?" is a question I incessantly ask my husband. I ask it so often, poor John must be tired of answering.

It wouldn't be so bad if he just had to come through with the expected, "Yes," in reply. But that's not enough.

It's impossible for me to fathom that anyone could find me lovable, so I then have to continue by asking the follow up question, "Why do you love me?" I can well understand why he finds that a tough question to answer!

I not only need to be told that I am loved, but also appreciate being the recipient of demonstrative love in action.

On a recent Sunday afternoon, John demonstrated his love beautifully. We had stopped at a shopping mall to eat lunch and go to a movie. After eating, but before the movie started, we had a little time to shop. John headed off in one direction to look at men's stuff, while I went the other way in pursuit of any really great buy.

At the appointed time, we met for the movie.

When it was over and we were strolling through the mall to get back to our car, I said, "There's a dress I saw I'd really like to show you. I kind of liked it and wondered if you would too. Do you mind if I show it to you before we go home?"

"Oh really?" John replied. "That's funny because I also saw a dress I thought you'd like."

I just knew he was joshing me. I couldn't imagine he would have taken time to look at dresses, much less find one he thought I'd like. Deciding to call his bluff, I coquettishly said, "Oh really? You show me the one you found first."

As we walked down the corridor, I tried to give no indication of what direction to head or which store was the one where I found the dress I liked. Yet, when we got to the correct store, John turned in and led the way.

I looked at him in disbelief when he actually headed down the correct aisle.

As I was thinking, "Man, this guy is really lucky to come this close," he proceeded to stop right in front of the T-rack where 'my' dress was on display.

After picking my chin up off the floor, I looked at John and said, "I can't believe it. That's the very dress I wanted to show you."

I went ahead and tried the dress on. After modeling it, John said, "Get it if you want it. It could be your valentine present." Instead, after realistic consideration, I hung it back on the rack. It was expensive and I really didn't need it. Besides, this demonstration of his love is a memory I'll always have to hold in my heart.

It's in the fabric of these seemingly simple day-by-day experiences that the tapestry of a shared love becomes evident. In life's common and unremarkable events, love has a way of weaving an all encompassing web of sustaining support to simultaneously utilize in times of trouble as well as times of joy.

❧ Mother-In-Love ❧

We all know our mothers love us. They *have* to because they're *supposed* to. But I'm lucky. I'm lucky because I also know my mother-in-law, Mable Keller, loves me. I know she does because, when I asked her to, she grabbed a handful of my hair and pulled it. But, I suppose I better start this story at the beginning . . .

Several years ago, John, Maury, Mickey and I went skiing with friends at Ski Cooper, near Leadville. Though we had skied hard all day, just as the lifts were closing, we couldn't resist riding up the slope just one more time for that infamous last run for the day.

Back then, I knew no fear. Swishing down a mountain at breakneck speed was daring and delightful rather than dangerous and dumb.

While on that final downhill run, I tucked tight, went as fast as possible, caught the tip of one of my skis, and fell.

John was behind me and saw me flip, fall, and land flat on my back. For a bit I just laid there, making no attempt to get up. Then, as John approached, with genuine concern he asked, "Jan, are you all right?"

"I'm not sure," was my dazed reply.

That evening, while traveling home, I said, "You know John, my neck is sure getting stiff."

A couple of weeks later I happened to go to the doctor. While there I mused, "Since I fell skiing, my neck has been bothering me."

The doctor felt my neck and had me move my head, but because I just mentioned it in passing, he didn't take it too seriously, and neither did I.

Over the next several months, however, my neck continued to bother me and strange things started happening. My arms increasingly became numb, and often I'd look down at my hands and fingers only to see them moving without my knowing it.

I was concerned when I returned to the doctor to complain about my neck, arms, hands and fingers. When the x-rays he ordered depicted nothing remarkable, I was referred to an orthopedic specialist.

For several months I wore a neck collar and popped pain pills and muscle relaxers. When those measures didn't relieve my mounting discomfort, I started making trips to a Colorado Springs hospital two or three times a week for outpatient physical therapy -- all to no avail.

Just as the ski slopes were opening for the next ski season, I was admitted to the hospital. After spending a week in traction with no improvement, a neurosurgeon was called in and a myelogram ordered.

I was terrified. I didn't think having dye injected into my spinal cord sounded like fun. Once the dye was injected, I was restrained and held motionless while being turned every which way, even upside down, while x-rays were taken. After all that was completed, the dye had to be removed.

After the doctors conferred, I learned I really had almost broken my neck skiing. One of the discs in my cervical spine was emaciated and protruding. Surgery was ordered.

I can't describe the emotions I felt as I signed the release papers on the night prior to surgery. Realizing one slight slip of the knife could result in paralysis made it very difficult to get a good night's sleep.

It was the day before Thanksgiving when I was wheeled down the hall and into the hospital's surgical suite. The holiday was a blessing. The surgery schedule was light and I only had a day to contemplate all the frightening possibilities. While counting backwards from one hundred, I went to sleep.

My next recollections were back in my own hospital room. Night had come and my room was quite dark. It seemed impossible to move my head. A humongous bandage was around my neck. But, most of all, I was thirsty. Very thirsty.

That's when I asked my mother-in-law to help me raise my head so I could take a sip of water.

I remember she looked down at me bewildered. She would gladly oblige, if she only knew how.

We tried a couple of different tactics to get my head elevated, but to no avail. My neck simply didn't seem able to support my head.

Finally, in desperation, I said, "Pull my hair."

Mable looked absolutely anguished by my request. To deliberately inflict pain on another is simply no part of her character.

I know it would hurt if just a little of my hair was pulled. But, if she pulled a whole handful, it wouldn't be bad. To demonstrate, I grabbed a fistful.

As she followed my example and pulled my hair, my head raised up off the pillow. At last I was able to take that memorable and intensely desired drink of water.

This incident taught me how very fortunate I am. I have a mother-in-law who is also a mother-in-love. She would do *anything* humanly possible to help me.

How lucky can I get?

❧ Remembering ❧

*I*noperable cancer was the diagnoses.

The public's response was an outpouring of hundreds of thousands of cards and letters, all with one thing in common: love for a man they had never personally met.

The man, television personality Michael Landon, touched the lives of common people with family programs.

Because I, too, was touched by this man's work, I tuned in to watch the television tribute, "Michael Landon: Memories With Laughter and Love," and learned he left behind quite a legacy. Throughout his lifetime, Michael Landon wrote one hundred and seven hours for television, directed two hundred and eight hours, produced three hundred and thirty hours, and starred in over eight hundred hours. His story themes were capable of bringing laughter as will as tears, while allowing viewers to get in touch with their own buried feelings and emotions.

Thanks to those hundreds of thousands of well wishes from fans, Michael Landon died with the knowledge his life had in fact touched others and made a difference.

Most of us aren't that fortunate. Though we live our lives from day to day, meeting and greeting and interacting with others, it is rare for anyone to express to another just how much their influence and friendship is valued.

Somehow, strange as it may seem, one day while enjoying lunch in a favorite Mexican food restaurant with Jim and his family, our conversation evolved to death and dying. Without a thought to the morbidity of the subject, I proceeded to say, "Well, when I die, instead of a funeral, I want a party in a beautiful grassy meadow, with good food, great music, and, most of all, balloons. Red balloons. That way, people could write the things they wish they'd said on a piece of paper and just let it go."

Then, in all earnestness, I looked at Jim and said, "And, if my body is so smeared it can't be willed to science, I'd like you for a pallbearer."

After this initial conversation, I realized, in addition to Jim, there are three other friends I'd particularly like to have carrying my weight after I'm dead and gone. I wanted to personally tell them of my wishes in an effort to express my gratitude for the way each nurtured the deep-down-inside real 'me'. Often it's been the friendship of these special people that kept me striving to do my best. Because each of them took time to smile and show they cared, my world has indeed been better and brighter.

A few weeks passed before I happened to talk to Hank on the telephone. While I stammered through what I wanted to say, I heard nothing but total silence. When Hank finally did respond, I heard a smile in his voice. I could tell he was pleased as well as overwhelmed.

"You know," said Hank, "I'm always dealing with the legal details of death and it has never been pleasant. But this -- you just made my day."

Next I told Keith. When I happened to run into him in the grocery store, ironically in front of the cold meat case, I said, "Oh Keith, I've been waiting for a chance to tell you something . . ." As I proceeded with my proclamation, a warm and knowing smile spread across his face. With Keith, I have talked of subjects related to death before. I know he believes in advance planning and communication. Keith communicated all that needed to be said with a warm and compassionate hug.

Even though I've seen Richard on several occasions, it never seemed the appropriate time or place for the conversation I had in mind. Finally, knowing this was the column I was to write, I picked up the telephone and gave him a call.

"Are you ready for what I'm about to say?" I asked.

"Should I sit down?" Richard responded.

⧽⋄⧼

I hope when I expressed my wishes to each of these kind and gentle men, they realized, in my own crude and clumsy manner, I was attempting to pay them the ultimate compliment. For other than my family, they are among the friends I'd want in attendance, someday in the hopefully distant future, for my final farewell.

I'd want them to enjoy the food and the music and the red balloons. And, in the words of Michael Landon, when that time for remembering comes, I'd want them to:

Remember me with smiles and laughter,
For that's how I'll remember you all.
If you can only remember me with tears,
Then don't remember me at all.

❧ *The Game Of Life* ❧

The lengthy Christmas holiday from school provides a wonderful opportunity for families to sit down and try out any new games left behind by Santa.

The name of the game at our house is Nintendo. It's an electronic system played on a television screen by means of hand-held control units. Though we've had Nintendo for a year or two, Christmas is an excuse to acquire more game cartridges. Even though John, Maury and Mickey spend hours and hours beeping, zapping, and scoring with their Nintendo, I've never touched a control. Why, I'm still intimidated by my microwave!

I personally prefer the more leisurely interaction between young and old that's possible while playing traditional games. Games everybody's played. Games like Monopoly, Scrabble or Old Maid.

It wasn't only during vacations from grammar school that Granddad Goldsmith could be counted on to play games. He loved to play games with his grandchildren. Because he did, sitting down together around the big dining room table was a frequent treat all the year through.

It wasn't hard to get a consensus about which game to play. In the first place, my grandparents didn't have many games to choose from. In the second place, Old Maid was the indisputable favorite among all the grandkids.

This past Christmas I never heard a single commercial touting Old Maid as *the* game all children just *had* to have. It's been years since I've heard anyone make mention of Old Maid, much less seen a deck of Old Maid cards prominently displayed in a store. Maybe that's too bad. Though politically incorrect, Old Maid remains a great game for children of all ages!

To play, all you have to do is pick a card from the hand of the person on your right. If it matches a card in your hand, lay the pair down. Then proceed on around the table by allowing the person on your left to draw a card from your hand. The object of the game is to match all the cards in your hand and run out. The problem is there's a one-of-a-kind Old Maid somewhere in the deck.

Eventually the Old Maid will be the only card left without a mate. Who ever ends up holding this one and only card bearing the likeness of an eccentric spinster looses the game and becomes the Old Maid.

It was especially fun to play this game with Granddad. Granddad *always* seemed to end up with the Old Maid. We thought he didn't understand the game or how it was supposed to be played.

"Granddad's the Old Maid," we would gleefully say to each other. Then, while we laughed out loud, Granddad would sit there with his dignified straight face that all but masked the twinkling in his eyes.

It wasn't until I got a little older that I began to notice the twinkling in his eyes. That's when I realized Granddad had really known how to play the game all along. For him, the pleasure of the game wasn't in winning. Instead, he was delighted by the young and innocent faces looking up to him from all sides of the table.

When I got a lot older, I realized Granddad had lived his life in much the same manner as he played Old Maid. He was always a willing and eager participant, never cheated, and, no matter how the cards were shuffled or stacked against him, he played the hand he was dealt with dignity.

By losing at Old Maid, Granddad proved to be a vivid role model of how to be a winner at the game of Life.

✒ *Timeless Treasures* ✒

I knew, even before I got out of bed, what I was going to wear that Saturday morning to visit Esther Fortenbaugh. On this day I would wear the wool plaid men's sport coat I purchased at the Goodwill Store.

I bought the jacket so I could sew on various hodgepodge of bobbles, transforming it into my own unique one-of-a-kind creation. Since buying and refurbishing the cast-off coat, Esther had been on my mind.

Esther moved into the new parsonage, just down the block from our house, with her husband Bob, who was pastor of the Calhan and Rush Methodist churches. Even though I know how Esther came to be my neighbor, I'm not sure why I'm so blessed as to count her among my friends.

On the surface it's apparent our ages and backgrounds have little in common. Upon closer inspection, however, one thing Esther and I do share is a desire to experience. Experience anything. Experience everything.

"I'll never forget the first time I was in your home," Esther recounted with a chuckle. "You were in the middle of making catsup!"

"Gee, I don't remember your visit," I responded. "But, now that you mention it, I do remember making catsup . . . But only once."

"I had never before known anyone who made catsup." Esther continued. "It made quite an impression."

"It certainly was an erroneous one," I concluded. "It was one adventure I never plan to experience again!"

Over the years, however, Esther and I did manage to find ourselves in many interesting adventures. Her husband Bob often referred to us as 'two peas in a pod'. Together we thought we could tackle almost any project. I've often wondered if Bob's description meant he thought we'd end up boiling in a pot of hot water together.

Esther rarely gave me material tokens of affection, and yet, I consider every gift she gave me to be priceless.

First there's the fist-size gray rock with intricate nooks and crannies, carved by the ocean's high and low tides. Esther scavenged it on some remote beach, right where nature deposited it.

She gave it to me after one of her trips to the east coast. That rock now sits on my desk at home, holding my pen.

Esther brought a most remarkable gift to cheer me in my hospital room as I was recovering from neck surgery. A rattlesnake vertebrae! To this day it remains adorned with the piece of green ribbon Esther tied through it and into a festive bow. I don't know where she found it. I don't know why she saved it. I only know I'll never discard it!

Then there's the small piece of driftwood. A beautiful, warm and knotty example of nature's ability to create one-of-a-kind unique designs.

"I can hardly wait to see what you do with it," were Esther's words when she gave it to me.

The years came and went. So did Esther. And, just as I couldn't forget her, I couldn't forget that piece of driftwood with its accompanying challenge. Even though time passed, I, too, could hardly wait to see what I'd eventually figure out to do with the gnarled and distinctive piece of wood.

Then came the day when I spotted that old wool plaid sport coat hanging on the rack in the Goodwill Store. Immediately I visualized the intrinsic beauty of my piece of driftwood adorning its lapel.

As soon as Esther and I greeted each other with a hug during my Saturday morning visit, she noticed my jacket and all the interesting things I had sewn on it. I was pleased to point out and make sure she recalled the focal adornment. It was important to me for Esther to see how I ultimately utilized her gift, and see its place of prominence and distinction.

Arthritis has slowed Esther up and made it increasingly difficult for her to venture out, but time with her always provides delightful and challenging stimulation because of her love of wonder, the undaunted spirit with which she faces life's challenges, and her unquenchable childlike appetite for what-next.

Esther is a lady who finds joy by living every day to the max and is as timeless as the treasures she bestows.

❧ Last Times ❧

I've always appreciated the mystique and charm created by the mere mention of past Christmases, birthdays, or any other special occasion celebrated together with family and friends. But since the death of my mother-in-law, Mable Keller, I've done a lot of reflecting. Reflecting on all the recent events that have been transformed, with abrupt suddenness and a deluge of emotion, into priceless memories.

I remember the bittersweetness of last Christmas. It was a wonderful day. Full of feasting, family and festivities. Yet, because of the reality of Mable's recently diagnosed cancer, just beneath the surface of conscious awareness lurked the demon of death, who we all realized could strike in the foreseeable future.

Following what had been a fun-filled day, Mable gave each of us a hug and a kiss as she was preparing to leave for home. It was then, as I watched Mable collect her dishes from the kitchen, that I saw how hard she was struggling to hold back her tears. I sensed she was wondering if this Christmas would prove to be the last time she would have a physical presence at Christmas celebrations.

This past and final Christmas also happened to be the last time I saw Mable adorned by her own hair. For, by the time a week had passed and the New Year arrived, chemotherapy had played one of its predictable and typically nasty tricks.

When we went to visit on New Year's Day, Mable greeted us at the door wearing her new wig and looked at if she wanted to break down and have a good cry. The tension of the moment was broken when she melted into my arms saying, "If you want to see my hair, it's in the bathroom wastebasket."

That was the last time I ever saw her cry.

Many of the last times I remember were ordinary and typical. Commonplace. At least they seemed common at the time.

The last time she visited our home. The last time she cooked us a meal. The last time we talked together on the telephone. The last time we got a note from her in the mail. The last time I saw her sitting in her recliner, busying herself with her handiwork.

The last times I remember go on and on, and yet, there is one last time I especially like to think about -- the last time I saw Mable smile.

It was the Saturday, one week after she walked with help into the hospital for what would be the last time.

It had been a week which brought with it rapid physical deterioration. Her arms had become useless attached appendages that no longer responded. While family and friends took turns being there to lovingly feed her, Mable's own arms and hands lay heavy and motionless at her sides.

Her legs, too, fell victim to cancer's vicious attack. No longer could they stand in support of her weight. They couldn't even change their position under the covers on the bed.

Her vision had dimmed so much that the big schoolroom type clock could no longer be read. Hauntingly it hung on the wall in her hospital room, constantly ticking away the moments we had left to spend together.

The relatives who had gathered for one final visit filled her room and overflowed out into the hospital corridor. Instead of being clear and distinct individuals, they had become shadows, recognizable to Mable only by the voices that accompanied them.

It was into this setting that one of Mable's nephews brought his beautiful baby granddaughter for a get acquainted visit.

As all of the dozen or so relatives gathered in the room and around Mable's bed took joy and delight in the baby, someone looked at me and said, "Take the baby close so Mable can touch her."

Obliging, I picked up the baby and carried her close to Mable, where I held the infant up over the rails of the bed. Then, to allow Mable to feel the baby's presence, I firmly grasped her lifeless right hand and tried to awkwardly raise it up toward the baby's head.

The baby, who wasn't a bit happy about being interrupted in the middle of a bottle, decided to voice a loud protest to all this commotion by starting to cry.

At that moment, in response to a sound ringing clearly with promise for the future, an unmistakable and memorable smile spread across Mable's face and brightened her countenance.

Realizing how difficult and different life is going to be now that Mable is gone brings tears to my eyes and makes me want to cry. But then, through my tears, I catch sight of a rainbow. This rainbow of promise for the future comes in the form of my memory of the last time Mable smiled. By smiling in the midst of her personal pilgrimage through the valley of the shadow of death, it was as if Mable gave a sweet benediction to life and all it represents.

⋅❧ *Big Trouble* ❧⋅

First came the clouds.
Then the wind and the rain.
Finally the hail.
This storm brought *big trouble*.
The date? June 6, 1990
The time? Approximately 8:10 p.m.

That's when the tornado dipped down, out of the sky, and indiscriminately struck Limon.

After the storm passed, the community was bombarded by the media. Each television and newspaper reporter who arrived on the scene wanted to interview anybody 'official' and be the first to get the scoop.

It's been years since this tumultuous event, but still, time in Limon can most easily be measured in terms of BT (before tornado) or AT (after tornado). For, with this one cataclysmic event, so many lives were picked up and twisted -- only to be strewn back down, shredded into mangled bits and pieces, and left facing various and altered directions.

Behind the scenes were many unsung and uninterviewed heroes who rolled up their sleeves and went to work. People who gave a hand and made a difference. One of these people is my friend, Jan Hiltner.

On that evening, Jan, a teacher, was one of four women attending an education meeting in downtown Limon. These women weren't aware of any imminent danger. They didn't hear any warning sirens. But, when torrential hail began beating the building, after looking out a window, decided to go to the far end of the building.

Then *it* came. The tornado.

From that moment on, it was Jan who remained calm. She's the one credited for talking the others through their frightening situation.

After the tornado passed, the women decided to get out of the heavily damaged building, that at least had succeeded in protecting them from physical harm. Looking around outside, in the overcast dusk of the stormy evening sky, they saw, and began to comprehend the magnitude of the tornado's destruction.

One of the women stayed downtown to help however possible.

The other three were married mothers, concerned about the safety of their families, and eager to go home. That, however, was no easy task. For, even if their vehicles would have been drivable, it was impossible to navigate safely through the devastation and downed power lines.

Thanks to assistance from others, the three women finally managed to get to Jan's house, just outside the northeast edge of Limon. Once there, Jan learned her family was safe, but their businesses, Limon Farm Equipment and Hiltner Motors, had suffered damage. Two cars from the car lot, that had been impaired by the storm, but were still driveable, were loaned to the two women so they could return to their homes in nearby Woodlin and Kit Carson.

After this nightmarish evening storm, the sun managed to rise on a new day. A day filled with work to be done, and a multitude of opportunities for friends and neighbors to help one another. The days that followed were long, hard, and exhausting, both physically and emotionally. Everyone became weary and worn out, eager for nighttime's quiet darkness, and the refreshing rest it provided.

Bright and early one morning, after two or three of these difficult days had passed, Hiltner's doorbell rang. When Jan answered it, much to her surprise, she found herself greeting one of the members of Limon's Town Council. He had come to enlist her participation on a tornado committee they were forming, comprised of a diverse group of Limon area citizens not personally devastated by the tornado, who would be a fair and non-biased representation of the entire community.

Jan was sought to serve on this committee because she was known to be levelheaded and thorough in making decisions. She, along with four other citizens, served on what came to be called the Limon Recovery Agency (LRA). These five board members were responsible for creating the organizational vision, and subsequent framework, for all relief and recovery efforts. They were the ones who administered all of the donations which poured in to assist victims and help with the cleanup. In addition they determined the guidelines governing the dispersal of funds, as well as how much money each applicant for assistance would ultimately receive.

At one time or another each member of the committee 'lost it' and gave in to the weight of the enormity of the task they faced. One of those times was during the *Up With People* concert. The LRA, feeling the community needed something upbeat and inspiring to bring everyone together and aid in the healing process, had arranged for this lively and youthful group to come and perform.

The night of the concert, however, the LRA was meeting. This committee, comprised of people who needed healing as much as anybody else, was off in a separate room, attending to business and making necessary decisions. Finally, just in time for the final song, the LRA members were able to slip into the gym and join the rest of their community. It was then, when Jan saw her family sitting there, without her, that tears filled her eyes.

Suddenly she felt torn. Didn't her physical presence and emotional support belong first and foremost with those she loved? Could the time she spent serving on this committee really make a difference for the whole?

Now, in retrospect, it's easy to see Jan's efforts did make a difference. When there were controversial or delicate issues with hard questions needing to be raised, Jan typically was the one who braved any possible subsequent peril and spoke up to voice them. She also had the ability to tactfully talk to people, encouraging them to apply for funding. She told them the money was there to be used. That it wasn't charity. It was help, freely offered, to anyone with a need -- whether that need was a new home or a new screen door.

Two years after the tornado, the LRA was officially dissolved. An estimated $400,000 in donations were dispersed. Their appointed task, completed.

Each LRA member has a story of their own. Each contributed and made a 'big picture' difference in their community's struggle to rise up from catastrophe and face seemingly insurmountable challenges. I've written about Jan Hiltner because she's the one I personally know. Maybe her story will raise awareness that communities all across the country, after being struck by natural adversity, have benefited from the time, energy, and talent of countless volunteers. Jan is just one of them.

Jan isn't a person who seeks attention or recognition. When she reads this story, I fear a different kind of storm will rage, and I'll find myself in *really big trouble*!

Note: Special thanks to LRA Chairperson, Susan Sparks, for information included in this story.

✎ *Lollygaging* ✎

*I*t's almost the Fourth of July.

It hardly seems like summer started, yet we're about ready to celebrate our country's independence. That means the county fairs are right around the corner. Then, in no time, it will be time for school to start up all over again.

The way time seems to fly, it's important to enjoy the remaining sunny summer season with fun-filled days spent enjoying family and friends.

When I plan a fun day, I usually set my sights on some special and fun destination. Sometimes it's the zoo. Other times, Elitches Amusement Park. Or it might be getting wet and wild at Water World. While recently enjoying a fun day with my young friends, Stephanie and Erin, I was reminded of a simple truth.

We started our day by taking a walk along a tree-lined stretch of the Big Sandy basin. Next we went to Limon's tennis courts, laced up our skates and then let 'em roll. Before long we got hungry, so we stopped for a refreshing lunch break. After appeasing our appetites, we went back and skated some more. When some tennis players came to use the courts, we decided to head for the bowling alley. After bowling a couple of games, we returned to the Big Sandy basin, where we ended our fun day with another walk.

The girls and I were in no hurry.

We had no deadlines to meet, or schedules to keep.

The day had been purposely set aside for lollygaging to our heart's content. And outside, in the grandeur of nature, that's exactly what we did. Lollygag.

We watched ants.

We looked out for clumps of cactus (but not nearly so closely as we zigzagged to avoid stepping in the middle of numerous other clumps).

We discovered a special strain of grass that could be pulled apart and put back together, kind of like pop-beads.

We picked several varieties of vividly colored wild flowers.

We got down on our hands and knees and let the sandy river-bottom soil filter, grain by grain, through our fingers.

We found the bony remains of a cow carcass, as well as the tracks of many of the species of wildlife who make their home in the area.

Along the way, in the midst of some of nature's most interesting settings, the girls posed to have their pictures taken.

As Stephanie, Erin and I headed back toward my car, Erin piped up and said, "Gee Jan, I didn't know you could be this much fun."

That's when the truth hit me. Fun days aren't necessarily about going places or spending money.

They're about lollygaging.

⚬ Joanna ⚬

 "*I*'m sitting here at the hospital looking out of the window and reading my Bible, and I needed to write you a quick letter," wrote seventeen year old Joanna Terry early one April. "I wanted you to know that Mom and I will be fine. I know our illness is very hard on you, but whatever has happened and will happen is God's will . . . We have to stay joyful and trust in the Lord. We all have our down days, but try not to get too depressed for a long time. Depression is so senseless. It accomplishes nothing and it just makes you feel bad. I'm not telling you to deny your feelings, but just give them to God."

Even though Joanna was seriously ill, thinking first and foremost of another, she was trying to comfort her father and bolster his spirits as he dealt with tumultuous stress.

The ordeal began on July 5, 1991, while Joanna and her family were spending the Fourth of July holiday at their mountain cabin near Buena Vista. Joanna and her father were out walking when she, a seemingly healthy member of her school's swim team, noticed and complained about a pain in her left side.

At first a pulled muscle was assumed to be the cause, but as the pain increased in severity her family decided to return home.

Because the doctor detected a large mass, Joanna found herself hospitalized. After seemingly countless tests were completed, the large lump near her kidney was believed to be a cyst.

Joanna was sent home with medication to shrink the lump, but to no avail. Because her pain was increasing and becoming intolerable, she underwent surgery to remove the lump.

The outcome?

Joanna's tumor was malignant. She did in fact have cancer.

On September 10, 1991, two days after Joanna's seventeenth birthday, she started chemotherapy. It was a grueling treatment cycle of multiple drugs, extended hospital stays and the predictable hair loss.

Just how does a high school senior deal with a bald head?

Joanna's method of dealing was with a dose of humor, saying, "God made only a few perfect heads -- he put hair on the rest."

Instead of a normal senior year, Joanna focused on hospital visits and doctors rather than parties, football games, dates and dances.

Then, as if Joanna's health wasn't enough to deal with, in October her family was dealt another devastatingly nasty blow. Her Mom, Joyce, was diagnosed with breast cancer.

For the Terry family, cancer was no longer someone else's mysterious disease. It was a fact of life. Their life.

Instead of becoming discouraged by all the sickness surrounding her during hospital visits, Joanna tried to stay upbeat and happy.

"I really feel lucky," said Joanna. "I see so much suffering at the hospital that I thank God I have so much support and am able to keep up with my life. If I can stay positive, maybe I can help others through a hard time."

She even wrote herself one powerful prescription: "Smile a lot. Don't get down. And don't get depressed."

Finally came graduation day. Wearing the traditional gown and an untraditional bandanna (to cover her baldness) Joanna, one of the top students in her class, stood before her peers, telling them, "Our daily actions and values are what make us worthwhile. I have really learned that a kind word or a pat on the back has unlimited value. Helping someone in their life and finding fulfillment in my own life means a lot more to me than a lump of green paper."

Only twelve days later, Joanna told her parents she felt a "catch" in her side. Soon it was confirmed. The tumor had grown back.

On July 2, 1992 Joanna, once again, underwent surgery -- this time at a Denver hospital. Her tumor was removed, but it was a difficult procedure. In addition to her kidney, the tumor had attached itself to her stomach, diaphragm and spleen.

Joanna left the hospital seventeen days later and went home to recuperate. But, instead of feeling better, she began to feel pain in her right side. Tests confirmed their fears. The cancer had spread there, too.

Joanna celebrated her eighteenth birthday on September 8. Although it proved to be a difficult day, Joanna, her parents, and brother found themselves supported and surrounded by a houseful of bright balloons, that seemed to multiply and keep on coming. The balloons, so symbolic of Joanna's light and bright spirit, were gestures of caring, tokens of affection, and expressions of love. They were gifts sent by a vast array of people. People who included friends, old and young; neighbors, near and far; doctors and their nurses — and even other cancer patients.

On Sunday, September 20, Joanna Lyn Terry departed this live.

Her memorial service was held the following Thursday. At its conclusion, the gathered throng of mourners went outside the First United Methodist Church in downtown Colorado Springs and released balloons into the air to symbolically let Joanna's spirit soar.

And soar it did.

I caught wind of Joanna's powerful story of faith and perseverance only because of a series of coincidences. It seemed when people got caught in the updraft of Joanna's essence, her spirit circulated and mysteriously passed from one to another.

Joanna's life, and how she lived it, touched me. The rare beauty of her thankful spirit is an inspiration.

This year while celebrating Thanksgiving, think about Joanna and these words from her graduation speech:

Make the most out of everything. Make a difference each day. Life will obviously continue with its highs and lows, but what we make out of everything that happens is what counts. Believe me, each day is important. I've learned to appreciate all that I do and to keep my perspective. Instead of always focusing so much on activities in the future and thinking, 'When I'm twenty-one, I'll start living,' or 'When I have a family everything will be OK.' Or 'The grass is always greener later on,' let's wake up in the morning and say, 'Look at the beautiful sunshine. Look at the grass and the trees. Boy am I grateful for this day!'

The Mother Of The Groom

I t isn't easy being the mother of the groom.

I should know.

I've just been through it.

Maybe the job's so difficult because there are few, if any, notorious role models to emulate.

Steve Martin starred in the movie remake of *'Father of the Bride'*. Spencer Tracy starred in the original version. Because I had an engaged son, it was timely for me to see them both. My hope was to glean a few hints to help with the real role I was struggling to play.

I was wrong!

The mother of the groom was all but nonexistent in both flicks. Her only line was, "It's nice to meet you," as she was introduced to the bride's parents.

The movies seemed to mirror our world. I've noticed society makes little note of the mothers who produce the world's supply of male children.

I've felt pangs whenever I heard about an upcoming mother-daughter luncheon or fashion show.

I've taken note of numerous father-son affairs.

But the father-daughter dinners have been the most unfair of all.

Have you ever heard of a mother-son *anything*?

Is there nothing special and worthy of social recognition about the relationship shared between a mother and her son?

Early in the planning stages of my son's wedding, his bride-to-be and her mother kindly invited me to go along with them on a shopping expedition to a large bridal store in Denver to look at wedding gowns. We had a great day together, but most memorable were the words of the clerk, who advised, "The groom's mother is supposed to wear beige and keep her mouth shut."

Realizing there might be some merit to this unsolicited counsel, I found my focus turning increasingly towards me, instead of allowing myself to get all wrapped up in the planning of the wedding.

I shopped for, and found, my dress.

A few weeks later I located a necklace, bracelet and earrings, to adorn my dress. After a few days of consideration, however, I went back to the store for extra earrings. I wanted to remake them into matching buttons to sew on my dress. I searched for months for just the right shoes, and once I found them, my focus was on locating pantyhose that perfectly complemented the color of my dress.

At Saks Fifth Avenue, just up the street from K-Mart, I fell in love with an exquisite ecru satin and lace handkerchief. But when I saw the forty dollar price tag attached to what in reality was a very beautiful fabric snot-rag, I turned and walked away. It wasn't many days later, however, when I walked into a fabric and lace store to purchase the necessary supplies to make a similar hanky.

Now my attention turned toward coordinating undergarments to complement my dress. Pretty dumb! Especially when I think about how mortified I would have been to have my slip actually show. Nevertheless, I searched for all the necessary garments so I'd be new, clear down to my skin, on the day my son would marry.

One might think there was nothing more I could do in preparation, but they'd be wrong. Now I began spacing my haircuts. The timing was critical to ensure my hair would be its best and most manageable for the actual day.

When the week before the wedding finally arrived, I turned my attention to all those last minute details. Each day I focused on my eyebrows. Painfully I'd pluck at any stray hairs that didn't conform or arch to suit me. It's a wonder I had any left!

It was two days and counting. This was the appointed time set aside for a new experience. I got my first set of artificial fiberglass fingernails. I was shocked to discover the application of phony nails take almost *two hours*! As I paid the manicurist for her services, she said, "If anybody asks if your nails are yours, say yes. You paid for them!"

Finally, after all this personal preparation, it was the day before the wedding. A busy day. A day set aside for setting up for the reception, wedding rehearsal, and the rehearsal dinner.

As the day wore on, I felt the need for a bit of time and space, alone. On the spur of the moment, instead of going to my son's apartment, where a horde of people were going to go to change their clothes, I decided to go directly to Shove Chapel. Even though it was an hour prior to the wedding party's rehearsal, I could get my clothes changed and then relax while listening to the musicians as they practiced for the ceremony.

In the chapel, while silently seated in a dark and obscure corner near the back, I took time to pause and ponder the wedding. It was now only hours away. And that's when it hit me. For more than a year, by busying myself with insignificant and superficial preparations, I had managed to mask and deny my emotions. As the sacred sound of beautiful music surrounded me, I got in touch with all I was feeling. By allowing my dammed up tears to freely flow, I released my reservoir of maternal tension.

అ~ఁ

The wedding day was blessed by bright and beautiful sunshine.
It was a time of joy.
The smile on my face was heartfelt and genuine.
At the appointed hour, as other eyes were on the bride, two soft and misted ones were on the groom.

❧ Budding Possibilities ❧

The large blossoms are beautiful and breathtaking. Almost shocking. The red lily-like petals, with an eight-inch trumpet-shaped span are an unexpected, though welcome, burst of color in the midst of winter.

Mom planted the amaryllis bulb in November and gave it to me Thanksgiving Day. When I first looked at the planted bulb, it didn't look like much. I could've believed it to be a clump of rotting tree bark.

The potted bulb was placed in my bedroom, where light and humidity would provide necessary elements for optimum growth. I even remembered to give it drink of water, once or twice a week.

For what seemed an eternity, I thought I was doing something wrong. Nothing happened. The bulb just sat there. Ugly.

It was supposed to bloom for Christmas -- but Christmas passed.

After almost giving up and throwing the pot in the trash, one morning a bit of a green shoot provided hope. Every day after that, the stalk grew stronger, though obviously not beautiful. Just a pot with one tall shoot. I was glad to keep it hidden in the bedroom, out of sight.

The bare stalk eventually grew to be three feet tall, then stopped growing. The bud at the top began to slowly swell. I became impatient. I wanted to peek at the blossom that was about to burst into bloom.

On a January morning, while leisurely laying in bed viewing the majestic red flower that finally emerged from the once dead-appearing bulb, our telephone rang. My husband John answered it, but I could tell it was Jack Lawson. Jack was calling with news. He and his wife Joan were the proud parents of their long-awaited baby girl.

Later that day I cradled newborn Lindsey Jo Lawson in my arms. She appeared a wondrous perfect vision of budding possibility.

Gazing at this beautiful new baby, I caught a glimpse of the promise and potential growing and developing within her being. I also thought of my beautiful red amaryllis blooming at home. I couldn't help wondering how many little babes, even when provided an optimum environment, somewhere along the way, just give up. How many quit growing and developing before achieving their ultimate destiny?

How many of us never fully bloom?

❧ *Unfinished Business* ☙

On my way back home after an overnight trip to Fort Collins to visit my son Mick, who attends Colorado State University, I realized the day ahead of me was virtually unplanned. Because I was by myself, I could do whatever my little heart desired.

❧❦☙

I've always planned to will my body to science by becoming a cadaver at Colorado University Medical School. Several months earlier I had called the facility to request current information and forms. When the packet from CU arrived in the mail, the information indicated that somewhere in the Medical School complex is a room set aside as a memorial to all the individuals who have been body donors. In the room is one large memorial plaque with small individual brass plates hanging from it. Each plate is engraved with the name, year of birth, and death of a specific donor.

When I first read this bit of information, I immediately stopped, paused, and went back to reread it.

❧❦☙

Today it's unusual for a person to donate their body for research or organ transplant. It was even more so when Dad informed us that was his desire.

Dad had Rheumatic Fever when he was a child. As a result, his heart valves were damaged and needed to be replaced. His surgery was November 9, 1966. I was seventeen-years-old at the time and vividly recall the day.

It was late that afternoon before the doctor came to talk to those of us who had idled away the day in the hospital's waiting room. The grim news was that Dad had not survived the procedure.

My dad was dead.

That's when my Mom signed the donor card and made Dad's expressed desire the legal course of action.

＊＊＊

My morning drive back home from Fort Collins was pleasant. It was a beautiful early spring day. All the way I pondered how to spend it.

With no definite destination in mind, I took one of the I-25 exits leading toward downtown Denver. I meandered past Larimer Square, the Tabor Center, the Denver Art Museum, but didn't stop at any of them. I continued east on Colfax, past the State Capital, and when I got to Colorado Boulevard, I turned south. Soon I passed the CU Medical School complex.

That's when my destination was suddenly decided and I turned around and went back.

After parking my car, I somehow managed to make my way to the chapel. It didn't take me long, however, to realize this wasn't the place I was looking for. I would have to ask for assistance.

The ladies at the information desk were very helpful, but they kept passing me on from one to another. It seems none of them had ever before been asked about a memorial room, somewhere in the complex, honoring the people who had served as cadavers. Finally, in desperation, one of them picked up the telephone and placed a call. After the conversation ended, she looked at me and said, "A lady is on her way to take you there."

When the lady arrived, we introduced ourselves, then the two of us took off, surrounded by an uncomfortable strained silence. After climbing a flight of stairs and walking down a hallway, we crossed a street in an enclosed overpass. We went down yet another hall before finally reaching an elevator. When we got out of the elevator, we walked halfway down a narrow corridor toward an open door.

The lady indicated I should go inside, saying, "This is the office. She can help you."

The woman sitting behind the desk looked up, smiled, and said, "I've been expecting you. They called to tell me you were on your way. How may I help you?"

Suddenly I was in touch with an emotionally charged connection leading directly into the past. This line, which I thought had been buried long ago, was suddenly surging with a live current that was shockingly painful.

When I started to speak, I found it difficult because my mouth seemed very dry and my voice wanted to crack. With great effort I briefly recounted the events from over a quarter of a century into my past. When I finished, I asked if there were any records of my father's death and donation.

The woman got up from her desk and left the room. When she finally returned, she held two cards in her hand.

As I looked at the two cards, I immediately recognized my mother's signature. She penned it long ago in a hospital waiting room to authorize Dad's body donation. The other card was a copy of my father's death certificate.

"That's all we have," said the woman as I looked up.

"In the information I got in the mail, I read that now the remains of the cadavers are cremated and buried in a Denver cemetery. Can you tell me what would have happened to my dad's?"

"That long ago," came her sure and steady reply, "the cremated remains were scattered on the grounds here at the CU Medical School complex."

After a long pause, I asked, "I would like to see the memorial room. Would you show it to me?"

She got up from her desk and led the way out of her office. I felt dazed as I followed her through a maze of hallways. After making several turns, we went down a dim corridor. The farther we went, the darker it seemed. Obviously, we were in some far removed and remote area of the building. A place the general public would not accidentally find.

Finally my guide stopped, reached into her pocket, pulled out a key, and unlocked the door. After the door opened, she reached into the darkness and turned on the light. I could see the room was quite small; more like a closet.

As I entered, I noticed the interior was paneled with warm and beautiful dark wood. And there, on the wall I was facing, hung the large and ornate plaque. Surrounding it were the small engraved plates, each naming an individual donor.

"Why is this room located *here*?" I asked.

"Because it's next to the anatomy lab, where the work is actually done," came her direct reply.

After we made our way back to her office, I said, "When Dad died, I don't recall ever hearing about the memorial room, or the opportunity to order a commemorative brass plate."

"No," she answered. "The space wasn't set aside until several years later. Today there's even an annual memorial service. The families of all the previous year's donors are invited, along with the medical students who studied the cadavers. It's really quite a moving service."

"Would it be possible to have a brass plate engraved for my father, even though the room didn't exist when he died?" I asked.

"Certainly," she replied. "Many of the plates honor individuals who were donors prior to the inception of the memorial room."

With that information, I reached into my purse and wrote a check to cover the expense.

When I left the Medical School, I noticed landscaped areas where well-established trees and shrubs were getting ready for another summer growing season. As I looked at them, I realized I had celebrated a personal Memorial Day in the midst of what for me had become a hallowed and consecrated resting place.

My business there was finished.

❧

When, and if, I ever visit the memorial room again, I will be able to locate a small brass plate that reads:

Oliver Hastings Goldsmith
1922-1966

For Dad is one of many honored by the large plaque, bearing the inscription:

- In Gratitude -

They became teachers, in their way,
and all have benefited by what they taught.

❧ 𝓡𝓾𝓼𝓽𝓵𝓮𝓼 & 𝓡𝓪𝓽𝓽𝓵𝓮𝓼 ❧

"Give me a pound of summer sausage," I requested of Rick Cofer, as he manned the meat counter in Woolsey's Food Center. "I'm treating myself today."

"That's why we stock deli meats," replied Rick.

"Oh," I said, "I'm not talking so much about the summer sausage as the fact that today is the last day of summer. It's absolutely gorgeous outside so I'm taking my two pups on a special outing. Just the three of us are heading to Castlewood Canyon, southwest of Franktown."

"Is it a neat place to go?" asked Rick.

With my lunch provisions now packaged and in hand, I replied, "It's a beautiful state park, and not too far away."

When I got back home, I threw together a sandwich, prepared containers of drinking water for me and my dogs, grabbed the dog's leashes from the closet, and headed out the door.

I didn't have to coax Kirby (a white Bichon who's aggressive bark effectively disguises his wimpy cowardice) and Capri (a mostly white Toy Poodle who believes he's a raging bull and would eagerly match himself against any foe). The dogs were right on my heels, and not about to be left behind.

When I arrived at Castlewood Canyon I purchased my park pass, parked and clearly displayed the pass on my car's dashboard. I offered Kirby and Capri some water before heading on our way past the old homestead. By taking the path going near the crumbling remains of the humble abode, we split off on a trail leading across Cherry Creek, and up the other side to the towering rocky rim of the canyon.

There were no other cars parked at the trail head, so as soon as the dogs and I were well on our way down the isolated trail, I took them off their leashes, allowing them to explore the terrain. Always they remained close and would quickly come running if I got out of their sight.

The freeze-dried vegetation in the canyon was a glorious blaze of Autumn crimson and gold, making it possible for me to enjoy the crisp crunching sound of the rustling leaves as we made our way up the twisting trail. As the ascent became steep and required more exertion, I became all the more aware of the sun's bright, penetrating rays.

Once we reached the rocky rim, I went near the edge and

tentatively looked down over the valley below. But I didn't tarry there. I felt more secure away from the very edge, and on the well-defined trail.

Time spent out-of-doors, in one of God's glorious natural settings, can be both peaceful and exhilarating. It seemed like I was literally on top of the world. While soaking up the warm sunlight and deeply breathing the distinct aromas of nature, I communed with my Creator, as I walked the length of the canyon's rim.

When I reached the far end, the trail turned and headed down the canyon, toward the remains of an old collapsed dam. The descent was steep and rocky as the narrow trail switched back and forth across the side of the slope.

I was just rounding a corner of the trail when I suddenly became aware of movement near my feet. Because of my momentum and the steep grade of the path, I could only continue on. When I got myself stopped, I turned and saw a four to five foot rattlesnake coiling in the middle of the path, not more that twelve inches in front of the dogs.

In a split second, I assessed the situation, became terrorized, realized just how close I had come to experiencing the poisonous fangs of this slithering serpent, and feared for the fate of my dogs. It would be just like Kirby to bark and agitate this creepy critter, and for Capri to aggressively attack.

As I stood spell-bound, helplessly watching just a few feet away, I fervently and simply prayed, "Oh God!"

Miraculously, both dogs stood still.

Neither of them barked.

Then, after a few moments passed, the dogs slowly backed off and turned to head back up the trail. As they did, all at the same time, I kept a wary eye on the snake, looked around to check for other snakes that might, likewise, be sunning in the area, and tried to figure out how I could get Kirby and Capri down off the canyon's rocky rim, and back with me.

Up on the ridge, the dogs ran from rock to rock, trying unsuccessfully to find a place where they could come to me.

The snake, now feeling less threatened, relaxed a bit and started to uncoil to once again bask in the sun.

In a repeated circular motion, I looked over at the snake, all around the area where I was standing, and up at Kirby and Capri. I could see no way for me to safely climb to the dogs, the snake remained in the path, and I felt totally isolated and helpless.

Finally the dogs, becoming impatient with the situation, began lightly whimpering, as if begging for me to figure out a solution to our dilemma. My shuffling around on the nearby rocks and the dogs' whimpered barks once again alerted the snake. Immediately the snake recoiled and began rattling out its distinct danger warning. This time, however, when the snake relaxed, it slithered straight over a rocky ledge and out of sight.

As soon as I felt the snake was far enough away, I went back up the trail to reunite with my dogs.

As I saw it, we had two logical choices. We could go back the same way we had come, which was by far the farthest. Or we could continue on, down the obviously dangerous path. After taking a very deep breath, I decided to take the shorter but more dangerous route down off the rim of the canyon. This time we traveled slower, and I became even more keenly aware of every rustle of leaves. A cricket's chirping was enough to stop me in my tracks. And any nearby buzzing vibrations of a grasshopper were nearly enough to cause me to croak on the spot.

When we finally made it back down to Cherry Creek, instead of turning to take the trail alongside the water, as previously planned, I continued on toward the road. As we walked along the road to get back to our car, we came upon two bull snakes out sunning. Carefully, we kept on walking, just as far around them as possible.

More than two hours later, Kirby, Capri, and I were safely back to the car. My senses had been sharpened to the ultra-fine point of skittishness and I was ready to go home. I had heard more than enough rustles and rattles for one day!

It's What I Didn't Do

I first met Flo Jensen, and her husband Ken, when I worked at the local feed and grain cooperative. They had moved to this area from Denver in 1978 because they both battled lung disease. On the windswept prairie, away from the smoggy air of the big city, they sought a breath of fresh air and better health.

As long as I'd know Flo, she was almost always hooked up to an oxygen tank. If she went anywhere, it did too.

Boisterous might be a good word to describe Flo. According to the dictionary, boisterous means durable, strong, and rowdy. I guess all of those adjectives fit, especially if you add Flo's lively sense of humor. She used to accompany Ken on trips to the co-op to buy feed for their animals. You could hear her distinct, wholehearted and infectious laugh as soon as she came in the door. Then, with a twinkle in her eye, she'd lean over the counter and ask, "Have you heard any good jokes lately?"

Flo was not one to put on false pretense. She may not have been society's idea of genteel, but she was genuine. Flo was who she was, like it or lump it. I happened to like it.

❧❦

One day, I happened to see Flo's son, Kenny, at Calhan's Post Office. "How's your Mom?" I asked.

"Oh, she's in the hospital," was his reply.

"How's she doing?" I continued.

"About the same," Kenny answered.

❧❦

No matter how hectic life seemed, I should not have been too busy to spend a little time with Flo. She was more than a friend. She was my 'other mother'.

Flo, who usually didn't drive, was eager for opportunities to get out and mingle with people. I invited Flo to go along with me to various social activities. Once I asked her to accompany me to a mother-daughter affair as my 'other mother'. I didn't realize how much that pleased her until a couple of years later when she was entertaining the members of one of her clubs and asked me to come as her guest. That day she introduced me as her 'other daughter'.

∂∽∾

I was stunned one Sunday morning as I read the obituaries printed in the newspaper.

"John," I said to my husband, "Flo died."

∂∽∾

Flo attended a Valentines Day luncheon I hosted several years ago. After everyone arrived, I had each guest tell how they had met their mate.

Flo said Ken was in the Navy when he marched into her life, dressed in the impressive trappings of his military attire. It was love at first sight. One week later, May 28, 1948, they were married. Through the good and bad, their union lasted forty-four years.

Flo said, "Jan, that sure was a nice party," when she left my house after the luncheon. Then, as she started to walk toward the driveway, where Ken was patiently waiting in their car, she turned back and added, "You know, I really like nice things, and that was nice."

∂∽∾

"Do you know what you're going to do today?" my husband asked.

"I'm going to Flo's funeral," was my reply.

"You're driving to Denver?" he responded.

"Yes," I answered.

∂∽∾

Flo was sixty-six when she died. Life for her had not been easy. Her father had worked for a Denver newspaper. Her husband, a firefighter for the City of Denver, always worked another job of two on the side to keep their family sheltered, fed, and clothed. They were hard working people.

Flo and Ken had four children. Three sons and a daughter. Even after raising her family and moving to Calhan, several of Flo's grandchildren came to stay with her and Ken for extended periods of time. She was pleased to lend a helping hand that also got the kids out of the rougher and tougher Denver environment.

Two of Flo's grandson's participated in her funeral service.

Richard called Flo the "glue that held the family together." He went on to say, "May we all retain zest for life as Grandma did."

The day before Flo died, family members gathered in her hospital room and offered a prayer. "Grandma lifted her hands and said, "Lord, I love You,'" Gary recounted. "She was sure of the direction she was going."

Flo's funeral service was true to the lady being honored. Reverend George Berlin characterized Flo as a plucky optimist, a tiger, and a fighter. "You didn't want to cross her," he said. "She could be ornery. Flo once took a garden hose to a neighbor. But when she was a friend, she was a friend for good."

᠗ᢀ

After the service, I waited by the hearse for the family to accompany the casket out of the chapel.

When Ken saw me, he steered his wheelchair, and accompanying oxygen tank and tubes, in my direction. When he reached me, I leaned over and gave him a hug and a kiss.

"Thanks for coming," he said. "Flo always thought a lot of you. I don't know why, but then, can anybody explain the way of emotions?"

"I know she did," I responded, with tears streaming down my face. "I loved her, too."

᠗ᢀ

I now live with the guilt of a grievous sin of omission. It's not a matter of what I did. It's a matter of what I didn't do.

My last visit to Flo came too late.

❧ *Light & Love* ❧

very Christmas, except, of course, for the one when I had a bad case of the stomach flu, had been merry and magical. All six of them. And I expected my seventh to be the same.

For weeks, I'd been living on the adrenaline my system created in excited anticipation of Santa's arrival. I hoped and prayed he'd think I'd been good enough for him to bring my heart's desire.

When I went to bed that Christmas Eve, I had an especially difficult time going to sleep. The sugar plums that danced in my head were in brilliant eclectic neon color, with accompanying background music turned up to the height of my imagination. This extravaganza of my mind was more captivating and entertaining than any ever staged on Broadway. Finally, however, Mr. Sandman came onto the scene as master of ceremonies and transformed the animated visions of my imaginings into a dreamland slumber. Though he quickly introduced Winkin', Blinkin', and Nod, the trio didn't hang around long. For, in no time at all, I was wide awake and eager to get up.

It's important to know I was the daughter of a dairy farmer. A dairy farmer's life revolves around his cows. The cows were milked twice a day. Dad got up at three-thirty for the first milking, and usually came into the house for breakfast around seven a.m. He milked the cows again in the afternoon at three-thirty p.m., and was in the house for supper by seven p.m. Because of Dad's long workday, one cardinal rule in our home was that his time to sleep was an important commodity that was to be highly regarded and diligently protected. It didn't matter whether it was Christmas or an ordinary day. The cows had to be milked, and Dad needed his sleep.

This particular Christmas, my morning arrived very early. So early, Dad hadn't gotten up yet to go milk the cows. He was still in bed sleeping. I stayed in my bed just as long as I could stand it, but eventually my anticipation became too great and I quietly slipped out of bed. Up on my tip-toes, I carefully crept out into the living room, groping my way to the Christmas tree. I had to see what Santa had brought.

The house was very dark. So dark that when I finally made my way to the tree and sat down on my mother's brand new and first-ever wall-to-wall carpeting, I couldn't so much as locate my stocking, much less discover its contents.

I had a real dilemma!

I wanted to be able to see -- but I didn't want to turn on a light and disturb my father.

Suddenly I had what I believed to be an enlightened idea. I could get the gooseneck lamp from the piano and bend the light bulb down close to the floor so only a little light could filter out into the room. Enough to see what Santa had brought. Not enough to bother Dad.

As soon as I had my lighting system rigged, I dumped my stocking. Immediately I was captivated and totally engrossed in its magical contents.

The next thing I remember, Mom hurried into the room, sniffing the air, and exclaiming, "I smell smoke!"

When I looked down toward the light, I could see it was engulfed in a dark billowy cloud.

Quickly I grabbed the lamp and twisted its neck upright. Fortunately, the carpet hadn't ignited into flame. Unfortunately, a round, light bulb-shaped circle of blackened scorch was branded into my mother's new carpet.

When I looked up, I expected Mom to be all ready to lower the boom. I knew I deserved a wailing.

Though Mom was obviously not happy, much to my surprise, she didn't raise her voice.

Later that day, after it dawned on me that I wasn't going to be punished, curiosity got the best of me and I asked Mom, "Why?"

"Because it's Christmas," she replied. "I know you're sorry for what happened and feel bad enough already."

In retrospect, that holiday season brought personal enlightenment, and I began to grasp and understand what Christmas is all about. It's the year when I learned firsthand what it means to be saved from deserved punishment by the light and love brought into this dark world by the birth of God's Son.

❧ Colors & Crayons ❧

ven when I was an elementary school student, the stores displayed an enticing array of school supplies. Shopping for mine was an annual ritual and highlight.

On the first day of school, the first order of the day was to check out the other kid's school supplies, to make certain my selections were in line with the current craze. Did they have a regular loose leaf spiral notebook, or a zippered one? Had anyone actually convinced their mom they needed a protractor or compass?

Some of the kids always started the year with pencils imprinted with their name, but mine were always the standard yellow with #2 lead.

The biggest status symbol, however, was to be the one with the biggest and best crayon assortment. Mine never was. I dreamed of talking Mom into the super huge assortment, complete with stencils and crayon sharpener, but I never did.

After our negotiations ceased, Mom always made me feel very fortunate, indeed, to be the proud owner of a new pack of forty-eight crayons. I vowed I would take such good care of them, that the box they came in would last all year long. What a joke! Long before Christmas vacation, my crayons became a cigar box hodgepodge, with the 'new' definitely worn off.

I used some colors more than others. I liked red and picked it all the time. Blue, green, orange, and yellow also were favorites. Even drab old brown was necessary to color the bark on trees. My forty-eight-pack even included metallic gold and silver crayons, which sounded elegant and beautiful, but really weren't.

Before the school year ended, there was a great disparity in the size and shape of my crayons. Some were reduced to short stubs, while others hardly looked used.

I'm sure my gray crayon was among the ones that still looked new.

As a child, I didn't like gray because it wasn't very pretty or bright. As an adult, I've come to appreciate it. Thanks to the post-graduate school of life, the ultimate arena of hard-knocks learning, I now see gray as a vital color. Life is full of gray areas. Very little can be colored black or white, much less right or wrong.

I'm appreciative when friends don't expect me to be the infallible good guy, wearing a never dirty white hat. When I stumble, and maybe even fall, I need forgiveness and acceptance. Although I'll be the first to admit I'm flawed and full of fault, it's comforting to realize and know close friends tend to see my virtues as the foreground, and my black hat vices as a blur.

Although pure, bright, and vibrant colors may always be preferred, because I'm human and make mistakes, I've grown appreciative of gray.

❧ *The Sound Of Silence* ❧

I wasn't supposed to be there.
It was an event publicized for men only. But after the gathered group of Colorado Springs businessmen had filed through the buffet line, eaten their meal, and settled back to hear the speaker, I unobtrusively slipped into the back of the room. Quickly and quietly I made my way to an empty chair.

I wouldn't go out of my way to hear many famous athletes speak. There aren't many whose names I would even recognize. But, because this speaker's reputed sterling moral character has remained untarnished and free from blemish, he's a man I went out of my way to hear.

After being greeted with warm and welcoming applause, Randy Gradishar stood at the podium and began to speak into the microphone, saying, "Now that I'm no longer a paid professional athlete, I'd drive a long way for a free lunch."

With an opening quip about food, Gradishar, the once All Pro Denver Linebacker and present head of the Denver Bronco Youth Foundation, succeeded in relating to his audience on a universal level. Having captured everyone's attention, he told of Bronco owner, Pat Bowlen, phoning Colorado University football coach, Bill McCartney. "It was a miracle in itself to have an NFL owner calling a college coach," said Gradishar. "But, because *Sports Illustrated* had just published an article about numerous CU football players being in legal trouble, Bowlen wanted to offer support and help."

That telephone call resulted in Gradishar, accompanied by Bronco players Billy Thompson and Claudie Minor, making a trip to Boulder to meet with some of the CU athletes. The subsequent rap session was for the good, noble and worthwhile purpose of encouraging the young developing athletes to make the most of their afforded opportunity to attend college by playing football.

Gradishar, Thompson and Minor willingly gave of their time. They had a right to be proud of themselves and their effort.

At this point in his talk, Gradishar seemed to take a detour. Instead of continuing in the direction of all the good works of the public Randy Gradishar, he began relating to the audience about the private Randy Gradishar, the husband and father of three children.

"God doesn't care about Rose Bowls, Super Bowls, championships, and things like that," said Gradishar. "When we reach those pearly gates of heaven, I believe the question will be, 'What did you do with your family?'"

Gradishar, a man with the potential to positively affect the lives of countless young people, continued, saying, "Our kids need four things. They need our time, availability, consistency, and commitment."

That parenting advice was followed by an unnecessary and surprising admission of personal failure. "But how am I doing at it? -- Right now, not so good," said Gradishar. "I need to go back home and take care of my own house."

Gradishar then tied his feelings of parental failure together with his tale about the trip to Boulder. He told his audience he had felt a sense of accomplishment while driving home after talking with the CU football players. That good feeling, however, was quickly dispelled.

Upon arriving at his home, Gradishar was greeted by one of his children. As the child looked up to him, total disappointment radiated from the small face.

One simple, solitary sentence, "Dad, you missed my game," said it all.

Five utterly unforgettable words caused Randy Gradishar to reassess his priorities.

They also brought absolute and almost deafening silence to the crowd.

✎ *Ducky Deals* ✎

"Could I please borrow a baby chick to use during the children's sermon in church on Easter Sunday?" I asked Verne Bixler, of Colorado Agri-Feed. "I don't need to buy one. I just want to take one home for the weekend. I'd bring it back as soon as I could. I promise."

Verne gave me a grin, then turned to the fellows working behind the cash register and said, "Next week when Jan comes back, give her a baby chick. She'll bring it back."

The next week when I returned to pick up a chick, I was told, "Sorry Jan. All the chicks sold. All that's left are four baby ducks."

"Are they tiny?" I asked. "Tiny enough to fit in an old plastic egg that pantyhose come in?"

"Come on. I'll show you," came the reply.

We headed into the back room and lifted a large canvas drape that created a special environment for the tiny little feathered creatures.

"Go ahead and fish one out," I was instructed.

The anything but ugly little ducklings scurried every which way. Finally I caught the one that decided to go swimming in its water trough.

"Oh, he's so soft and cute!" I squealed.

My delight, however, was quickly replaced with remorse when an instant later the poor little creature, having fallen out of my hands, was lying in a dazed heap at my feet. After I picked him up, I said, "I guess I don't make a very good mama duck," as I held him closer and tighter than before.

"Come back just before you leave Colorado Springs to head for home," I was instructed. "We'll have you take a pair of the ducks because they're a flock animal and one usually doesn't do well."

Later that afternoon, I returned for the promised pair of ducklings, only to hear, "We sold one pair since you were here this morning and another one died. You'll have to settle for one duck because that's all that's left."

I didn't say a word, but felt guilty. I instinctively knew the duck that died had to be the one I accidentally dropped.

When I walked out of the store with a duck and enough feed to get me through the weekend, the fellows behind the counter hollered, "Good luck!" in a tone that sounded considerably less than optimistic.

಄಄಄

When I carefully carried my weekend duck into the house, he was making his presence known just as loudly as he could. I decided right then to call him Squawk!

In a flash, my dogs, Kirby and Capri, were on the scene barking and jumping, trying to see what was making such a racket inside the box.

I sat the box down on the clothes dryer in the laundry room and proceeded to rig up a light to shine down into the box to keep Squawk warm. I also rounded up an old alarm clock to tick and tock to the little creature to help it feel less alone.

Kirby and Capri were able to forget about Squawk until the first time I took the duck out of the box and they actually got a look at him. After that, the dogs spent hour after hour lying on the laundry room floor, patiently looking intently up at Squawk's box.

಄಄಄

On Easter Sunday, I quickly carried Squawk into the church and hid him. Fortunately, he kept still and his presence wasn't discovered.

When it was just about time for the children's sermon, I left the church service to go and get my feathered friend. It took longer than I expected because, just as I was trying to get Squawk settled into a plastic egg, the egg cracked. Frantically, I hunted for some scotch tape, but to no avail.

About that time my husband John came hunting for me. Realizing I had no choice but to get back into the sanctuary, I quickly handed my basket of eggs to my son's girlfriend, Amber, pausing just long enough to show her the cracked egg and ask her to bring me the basket at the appropriate time.

Once I settled, I began telling the children a story about the signs of new life. When it was time, Amber brought the basket of eggs.

Even though I wanted to open the egg with a purple crocus first, Squawk couldn't wait and immediately popped out.

Once church was over, I knew my time with Squawk was limited. Amber had fallen in love with the little fellow and had asked if she could keep him. I told her she could take him home after church.

With very little time left to spend with the duckling, I decided to take Squawk out in the yard and carefully let Kirby and Capri get a close look. Much to my surprise, the dogs were very good with the duck. The trio ran all around the yard, barking and squawking and carrying on.

Squawk went home to live with Amber, so I needed to settle my account with Verne at Colorado Agri-Feed.

Early Monday morning, I gave him a call, saying, "I guess I won't be bringing the duck back."

"What's the matter? asked Verne. "Did it die?"

"No. The duck is fine," I replied. "My son's girlfriend decided to keep it. I'll stop by soon to pay you."

A couple of days later I stopped by Verne's store with a check in hand to pay for two ducks -- the one I borrowed and the one I dropped. That was the only way I could ease my conscience and get out of this ducky deal!

❧ *Forever Amber* ❧

or the past couple of years, it seemed like Amber was forever at our house. Chances were pretty good that if our son Mickey came walking through the door, Amber would be following close behind.

From the very beginning of their courtship, Amber knew her presence was welcome in our home. If Mick liked her, we liked her. It was as simple as that.

No one is treated like a guest at my house for very long, so Amber quickly learned to fend for herself. If I was having one of my regular I-don't-feel-like-cooking days, she knew to make herself at home by rummaging through the cupboards or refrigerator whenever she felt hungry.

As the mother of only male offspring, I wasn't sure how to treat or relate to another female around the house. During one long day of Sunday TV football, Amber left the men glued to the tube and opted to help me work outside in my yard. That was when I realized having her around could sometimes mean feminine companionship for me.

About the time I was becoming accustomed to someone helping me set the table, as well as dig outside in the dirt, Amber did something that caught me completely off guard. As we were getting ready to go to a wedding, she came to me and asked, "Jan, would you help me with my hair?"

What do I know about styling long hair?

Absolutely nothing, that's what!

Yet, when I started to open my mouth to utter the simple truth, I looked into her trusting eyes and found myself saying, "Well, lets see . . ." as I pondered a course of action.

Amber must have been satisfied with the results because on numerous subsequent occasions she asked me to give her hair a finishing touch, add color to her cheeks by applying some blush, or dig through my jewelry for just the right accessory to complete her outfit.

I will forever remember Amber's senior prom. It was a night of an unexpected crisis. Amber came to me with tears brimming her eyes and said, "Jan, instead of a corsage, I wanted a beautiful dainty little floral bracelet. But look at it. It's so . . . so *big*."

I looked down at the floral mass, looked up at Amber, and then looked back at the flowers. To myself I though, "You guys are late, have no time to waste, and on a moment's notice, and I'm supposed to work a miracle?"

After a protracted pause, I took a deep breath and swallowed hard. Then, as I opened my mouth to speak, I was surprised to find myself suddenly inspired and said, "Why don't you open the bracelet and wear the flowers in your hair?!"

I knew Amber liked the idea by the radiant smile that spread across her face.

৵৽৹

One day in June, I was caught up in a crisis of my own. It was the day I learned a photographer from the Colorado Springs Gazette Telegraph was coming the following evening, right at sunset, to take a picture of me out somewhere on the expansive prairie around Calhan.

This time it was Amber who came to my rescue.

Patiently Amber tolerated and humored me as I tried on several outfits and ultimately helped me decide which one to wear. As soon as that decision was reached, I said, "Amber, I'm supposed to be thinking about an appropriate setting for the picture. Do you have any ideas?"

"Oh Jan, I know the perfect spot," Amber excitedly replied. "Out on soapweed Road, looking west, there's this beautiful rocky valley with one small butte in the middle of the pasture. Every time I drive past, I look and think how beautiful it is."

The next evening, Tom Kimmell from the Gazette arrived. Wearing the outfit Amber and I selected, I directed him to the little valley Amber had suggested. There, way out in the middle of a grassy pasture, surrounded by a herd of Holstein cows, I sat on a rock and posed while Tom set up lights and captured the moment on film.

When I got home, Amber and I giggled about my glorious evening in the limelight and the fun of pretending to be a beautiful cover girl. With anxious anticipation, I began eagerly waiting for the picture and accompanying article to appear in print.

৵৽৹

On Saturday, the first of July, when I turned to a new page on my calendar, I had no idea the day would unfold into such horrific tragedy. That afternoon, shortly after three, our telephone rang.

Mick was calling.

Amber and her mother had been struck by lightning while the three of them were playing golf. Amber had sustained a direct hit and no heartbeat or respiration could be detected.

Quickly my husband John and I got ready and headed to the hospital. Though we were in a hurry, the ensuing storm and accumulated hail made our going slow.

When we finally reached our destination, Mick was looking out the waiting room window. From his obvious despair, I could tell the situation was grim.

Before the sun had set, our worst fear became reality. Amber had passed away.

The days that followed were shrouded by the deep darkness of grief.

৵৵৵

A couple of weeks later, I was engulfed in a bleak and gloomy pallor, rather than ecstatic excitement, as I opened the newspaper and began to search for the visible result of my sundown session with Tom, the photographer.

When I found the picture, I saw my likeness sitting on a rock, dressed in the carefully selected outfit. There I was, surrounded by Holstein cows in the midst of an especially beautiful valley located on the expansive prairie off Soapweed Road, just outside Calhan.

As I looked at this picture directly influenced by Amber, I felt pensive and melancholy grief as my eyes drifted to the glorious glowing sunset in the background.

Now, whenever I look at this especially treasured picture, my memory will be forever Amber.

LIFE & LOVE
Look beyond the wholesome face
Friends forever will set the pace
Take a day and make a smile
Or just sit the night and cry for awhile.

Life is something to look forward to—
Love is the part that gives it to you.

A TRUE FRIEND
A friend is a sign of grace,
Someone who sees beyond the face.
Through the heartbreak, trouble and strife,
Someone who wants to be a part of your life.
A friend has a special kind of care,
An emotion and love they are willing to share.
Only a friend will see you through,
They will hold your hand when you are blue.
Someone who will be by your side until the end—
That is a true friend.

Poems and Drawing
by
Amber Fetters

MY LOVE
Although a flower may die,
love for you will never say goodbye.

"I love you and leave me never,"
se are the words I'll cherish forever.

Although a flower may die,
love for you will never say goodbye.

"Jan, your writing is so you — humor, tenderness, insight, vulnerability and, most of all, love. What a beautiful tribute to life!"

Dee Ring Martz, M.A., L.P.C.
Colorado Springs, Colorado

"I received Jan's book for my birthday and enjoyed it bit by bit as I stir the pots or wait in the car for the kids. Keep writing!"

Doris Heine
Vermillion, South Dakota

"Jan's writings are a delight to read . . . Sometimes I finish a page with a chuckle, and other times I put the book aside to appreciate her thoughts and observations."

Phyllis Erickson
Greenwood, Nebraska

"I found Jan's book hard to put down. Many things made me feel I had walked in her shoes at different times in my life."

Louise Holcomb
Cortland, New York

"What a delightful, interesting and heartwarming book. I enjoyed it so much. It's wonderful!"

Vicki Nelson
Loveland, Colorado

Jan Keller grew up on a dairy farm northeast of Greeley and has lived in Colorado all her life. She and her husband John reside in Calhan, right in the heart of the Pikes Peak Plains Region east of Colorado Springs. They are the parents of two grown sons. Because *The Tie That Binds,* was written a little bit at a time, that may be the best way to read it. The columns contained here and in her other book, *Pieces From My Crazy Quilt,* were originally shared with readers of *Ranchland News* between 1985 and 1996, and are now in syndication. You'll discover yourself in Jan's private, personal and poignant reflections and relate to the myriad of emotions she expresses. This book, a celebration of life and a gift of love, is sure to touch your heart.

Inquires Should Be Directed To:

Black Sheep Books & Publishing
P.O. Box 325
Calhan, CO 80808